THE ONCE AND FUTURE FOREST

THE ONCE AND FUTURE FOREST

CALIFORNIA'S ICONIC REDWOODS

Introduction by Sam Hodder

President and CEO of Save the Redwoods League

Includes essays by Gary Ferguson, David Harris,
Meg Lowman, Greg Sarris, and David Rains Wallace

H

Heyday, Berkeley, California

Copyright © 2018 by Save the Redwoods League
First hardcover trade edition, 2021

We are grateful to Anderson-Lovelace Publishers for underwriting the production of this book.

All rights reserved. No portion of this work may be reproduced or transmitted in any form or by any means, electronic or mechanical, including photocopying and recording, or by any information storage or retrieval system, without permission in writing from Heyday.

The Library of Congress has cataloged the original 2018 edition as follows:

Names: Hodder, Sam, writer of introduction. | Save the Redwoods League.
Title: The once and future forest : California's iconic redwoods / Save the Redwoods League ; introduction by Sam Hodder ; with essays by Gary Ferguson, David Harris, Meg Lowman, Greg Sarris, and David Rains Wallace.
Description: Berkeley, California : Heyday ; San Francisco, California : Save the Redwoods League, [2018]
Identifiers: LCCN 2018035684 | ISBN 9781597144445 (hardcover : alk. paper)
Subjects: LCSH: Redwoods—California.
Classification: LCC SD397.R3 O53 2018 | DDC 634.9/758—dc23
LC record available at https://lccn.loc.gov/2018035684

Cover Photo: Dale Haussner, Del Norte Coast Redwoods State Park, California
Endsheets Photo: Mike Shoys, Redwoods National and State Parks, California
Cover Design: Ashley Ingram
Interior Design/Typesetting: Marlon Rigel

Published by Heyday
P.O. Box 9145, Berkeley, California 94709
(510) 549-3564
heydaybooks.com

Printed in East Peoria, Illinois, by Versa Press, Inc.
10 9 8 7 6 5 4 3 2 1

FSC
www.fsc.org
MIX
Paper from responsible sources
FSC® C005010

CONTENTS

Introduction by **SAM HODDER,** President and CEO of Save the Redwoods League   1

DAVID HARRIS, My Redwood Confession   13

GARY FERGUSON, Guardians of the Giants   55

GREG SARRIS, The Ancient Ones   101

MEG LOWMAN, The Science of Giants   129

DAVID RAINS WALLACE, Redwood Time   161

Introduction
Sam Hodder

PRESIDENT AND CEO OF SAVE THE REDWOODS LEAGUE

Redwoods—our coast redwoods and giant sequoia—are among the most incredible living things in the world. Their forests have stood on this Earth for millennia, since long before humans evolved, bearing witness to time everlasting. To walk among them is to look upon the original face of nature and experience the incomparable majesty and beauty of the tallest and largest living things. Yet these stately ancient giants might have been lost forever had it not been for the dedication and passion of Save the Redwoods League, our partners, and community members who over the last century have made efforts to protect these forests.

Within the pages of this book, assembled to mark the occasion of the League's centennial year in 2018, we brought together five writers to share the remarkable story of redwoods in California, and the science, culture, history, and inspiration behind redwoods conservation. As I introduce the authors and the chapters to follow, I will share more about the occasion for which this book was produced and our vision for the future of the redwoods.

Coast redwood and giant sequoia forests are true wonders of the world. Each individual tree has the potential to stand for thousands of years, reaching heights unmatched by any living thing and volumes so large that they defy comprehension. These trees support rare layers of life found nowhere else on Earth, some in the highest reaches of their canopies. Redwoods can even play a significant role in slowing climate change, as they store substantially more carbon from the atmosphere per acre than any other forest the world over. They are ancient marvels to behold, and they have withstood eons of change.

Since time immemorial, Indigenous peoples of this land that we now call California have lived in close relationship with these forests, stewarding them with traditional ecological knowledge. We know some of these tribes today as the Sinkyone Tribe, the Yurok Tribe, the Tolowa Dee-ni' Nation, the Kashia Band of Pomo Indians, the Tule River Indian Tribe, and dozens more. European American settlement altered the future of those tribes as well as that of the forests that were fundamental to California Native peoples' identities, cultures, and histories.

In the wake of the 1849 gold rush and California's explosive

INTRODUCTION

demand for lumber, coast redwood forests that had flourished undisturbed along the North American west coast for more than two hundred million years—since dinosaurs roamed the planet—suddenly faced near-elimination. In just a few generations, the world's only native coast redwood range transformed from one massive, ancient forest ecosystem—stretching 450 miles from southern Oregon to California's Big Sur coast—to just 5 percent of its original extent. That's a loss of more than two million acres of ancient redwood forest in a matter of decades. Similarly, giant sequoia on the western slope of California's Sierra Nevada also suffered huge losses, with nearly a third of them slashed to the ground.

Fortunately, the visionary founders of Save the Redwoods League organized to safeguard these ancient and irreplaceable forests from the brink of extinction. They worked tirelessly to form what would become and has remained the world's first and only environmental organization devoted exclusively to the permanent protection of coast redwoods and giant sequoia across their entire natural ranges. Parcel by parcel and acre by acre, Save the Redwoods League has worked to protect the last of the world's ancient redwood forests and the surrounding young forestland needed to sustain them. In so doing, the League effectively played a monumental role in launching this country's land conservation movement. As our founders developed the tools of modern land conservation, they inspired a cultural shift in the country—a recognition that the value of our nation's remarkable forests extends well beyond their monetary value. Redwoods soon became emblematic of the American landscape, treasured for the forest's intrinsic ecological value and the psychological, emotional, and spiritual benefits of a simple walk in the woods.

Yet we at the League also acknowledge that along with their conservation achievements, our founders were also leaders in the discriminatory and oppressive pseudoscience of eugenics in the early 20th century—around the very same time they dedicated themselves to protecting the redwood forest. Today, in our second century, as we define the role we hope to play in a new conservation era, an honest reckoning with that past will be critical to a firm foundation on which to build a more inclusive future and begin the process of healing ourselves, our communities, and our forests.

As we reckon with, and learn from, our past, we also admire the extraordinary impact of those who have come before us. Save the Redwoods League—in close collaboration with landowners, donors, public agencies, conservation organizations, and other partners—has protected more than 218,000 acres of coast redwood and giant sequoia forestland. In that time, we have worked to create sixty-six redwood parks and preserves and to pioneer innovative, science-based forest restoration work. We have inspired millions of transformational experiences as generations of visitors from around the world have walked among the ancient, towering giants that we have

INTRODUCTION

protected. We have advanced scientific discovery in these forests and educated hundreds of thousands of schoolchildren about the redwoods' role in California's natural history, ecology, and future resilience. And by bringing together the greatest ecological minds to examine these forests from the ground level all the way up into the canopy hundreds of feet in the air, we have confirmed that redwoods are critical resources in our response to climate change.

Over the past century, we have learned a great deal about how redwood forests function; how quickly roads and clearcuts can jeopardize the health of our forests; how protected islands of redwoods remain vulnerable when surrounded by seas of barren cutover lands; and how, by contrast, sustainable timber practices can actually help redwood forests expand and thrive. We have also learned how redwood parks enrich our lives and make our communities stronger. And today, visitors to the redwoods have the opportunity to connect with a landscape unlike any other—one that embodies a sense of beauty, balance, and resilience millions of years in the making.

As we look to the future of redwoods conservation and the future of Save the Redwoods League—knowing that we have safeguarded much of what remains of the old-growth forest land—we must now turn our attention to securing the broader resilience and function of the redwood ecosystem. At the moment of our centennial, more than a million acres of redwood forest remained unprotected and primarily managed for commercial timber production. While forest practices have improved dramatically over the decades, much more should be done to regenerate a resilient and high-functioning landscape.

Meanwhile, our protected forests are often surrounded by land so degraded by past practices that it threatens their long-term health. Clear-cutting and thousands of miles of logging roads lead to erosion and runoff that strangle fish-bearing streams and threaten downstream groves. Ongoing drought, dense post-harvest thickets, and a century of fire suppression conspire to make our coast redwood and giant sequoia forests tinderboxes that would turn what would otherwise be a restorative ground fire into a devastating high-severity wildfire.

Furthermore, fragmentation, roads, and the disconnect between different forest management approaches that surround the redwood parks stifle the migration and limit the ranges of wild animals that have depended on healthy, intact redwood forests for their survival for millions of years. The world's last remaining old-growth redwood groves are isolated islands lacking critical connections to surrounding landscapes. The sea of young redwood forest that surrounds these islands is struggling in a downward spiral of perpetual recovery as the cycle of commercial harvest rotations suppresses its natural tendency to thrive, never allowing it to grow into a mature, healthy forest.

What the forest requires of us now is that we accelerate our conservation efforts—that we go big to ensure the vitality of this globally unique forest for future generations. In the next hundred years, the League will increase the scale and impact of our conservation work; our longstanding mission of protecting a healthy, vibrant redwood forest demands it. That is why the League, on the occasion of its one-hundredth birthday and at the dawn of its second century of conservation work, embarked on what we call a Centennial Vision for Redwoods Conservation, an outlook grounded in scientific research and decades of experience and dedication to protecting these lands.

> The Centennial Vision of Save the Redwoods League:
>
> *The League envisions a vibrant redwood forest of the scale and grandeur that once graced the California coast and Sierra Nevada, protected forever, restored to reflect the old-growth characteristics that were lost, and connected to the public through a network of magnificent parks that inspire the world with the beauty and power of nature.*

At its core, our Centennial Vision is about preserving these globally significant forests and the transformative "redwood moments" they inspire for generations to come. Redwood forests are among our holiest of places; they are where we go to renew our spirit and immerse ourselves in their silent beauty, to find peace and comfort in their unfathomable resilience, to gain perspective of and humble respect for their massive longevity, and to witness firsthand the irrepressible power of nature.

Together with landowners, supporters, and partners, we have set in motion the reclamation of the ancient redwood range and sow the seeds of a new old-growth forest that will help sustain the planet and inspire new generations of Californians and visitors of all backgrounds and identities. Moreover, we will renew our human connection to the natural world through the treasured gateways of our dedicated redwood parks—parks that belong to all of us and thus should be welcoming and resonant to our full community.

With the past at heart and our vision for the future of these forests in mind, we know that one hundred years is just the beginning of the League's work to save the redwoods. Inside this book, *The Once and Future Forest: California's Iconic Redwoods*, we hope to convey the history, iconography, science, and innovation that brought the League and our redwood forests to the pivotal moment where we stand today. To that end, we have brought together five prominent authors to share their stories and reflections.

David Harris, a notable author and former contributing editor to *Rolling Stone* and the *New York Times Magazine*, offers astute observations about the inspiration and iconography of redwoods in his essay, "My Redwood Confession." Beautifully written, emotive, and inspiring, this piece speaks to the importance of redwoods in our lives and personifies *Sequoia sempervirens* in a moving and insightful narrative. Harris's

"Seven Redwood Virtues" share what we can learn from these massive and resilient trees.

Gary Ferguson, a lecturer and best-selling science and nature writer, shares a new look at the history of the League. His essay, "Guardians of the Giants: One Hundred Years of Save the Redwoods League," is full of extraordinary anecdotes of early conservationists' work to protect coast redwood and giant sequoia forests. Ferguson takes readers on a journey from the League's modest beginnings, which started with a road trip up the Northern California coast to witness the destruction of redwood trees, leading up to the celebration of the League's centennial and one hundred years of protecting and restoring the tallest and largest forests on Earth.

Greg Sarris, an accomplished writer and the longtime chairman of the Federated Indians of Graton Rancheria, blends history, ethnography, and reflection in his evocative essay, "The Ancient Ones." Sarris provides rich detail of local Indigenous people's intimacy with and knowledge of redwoods and the California landscape, as well as the trees' significance in their lives and identities, while sharing the potent contrast of life before and after European contact.

Meg Lowman, a senior scientist in plant conservation with the California Academy of Sciences, takes a scientist's view of the League's leadership in redwoods research. She has spent her adult life studying one of the least explored areas on Earth—the topmost branches of redwood trees, reaching hundreds of

INTRODUCTION

feet in the air—and here she tells the story of the community of researchers that has revealed, and continues to reveal, the mysteries of the redwoods. Through her essay, "The Science of Giants," Lowman takes readers on an engaging journey, exploring the past and future of redwood science while providing a wealth of information and stories that educate and captivate.

Finally, David Rains Wallace, the author of more than twenty books on natural history and conservation, explores redwoods in the fourth dimension in his essay, "Redwood Time." This thoughtful and well-documented story examines the unique presence of redwoods as one of the oldest species on Earth, tracking their existence through time, from distant epochs through fossil records and up to the present day. His words connect us with the trees' past and offer a glimpse into their future.

I hope you enjoy these stories in celebration of our centennial. In the League's second century, I am honored and humbled to be the president and CEO of this remarkable organization. As I walk among the redwoods—these majestic "ambassadors from another time"—I breathe in the freshness of the air that they clean for all Californians and feel the moments of joy and inspiration that have accumulated across generations on the trails through these cathedrals of nature. Even so, as I read through the stories in this book, I am reminded that our work is just beginning, and that the urgency and relevance of our vision to heal the forest and keep it on a path toward recovery and resilience is our generation's greatest opportunity to leave the world better than we found it.

    Stand for the Redwoods, Stand for the Future
    One hundred years is just the beginning.

My Redwood Confession
David Harris

ME AND MY TREE

I am seventy-one years old, a fourth-generation Californian. As my life winds down, one of the companions I am most grateful to have had happens to be a tree, odd as that may seem.

It is not just any old tree but a very particular species, to be exact: *Sequoia sempervirens*, the coast redwood, the tallest of all, found only within forty miles of the Pacific Ocean along the California coast from south of Monterey Bay all the way north across the Oregon border, colonizing damp creases in the landscape, feeding off the winter rain that falls in sheets and the slabs of summer fog that make landfall every afternoon. It crowds the riverbanks of the Eel, the Navarro, the Russian, the Mattole, the Mad, and the Smith Rivers, as well as all the lesser watercourses that drain into them. If left uncut and to its own devices, this tree will grow as tall as 370 feet, longer than a football field, and almost thirty feet thick. And with a natural life span well beyond a thousand years, a *Sequoia sempervirens* is not even considered an adult until it reaches the age of four hundred.

That said, the only redwoods that remain unlogged and able to pursue adulthood these days are crowded inside one of some ninety Northern California parks devoted to the old-growth redwood's fragmentary preservation. These refuges collectively cover only a fraction of the coast redwood's native range, but on all sides of those enclaves, where once their trunks grew, every logged redwood stump sprouts a new tree—hence the name *sempervirens*, "always living."

In Humboldt, Mendocino, and Del Norte Counties, where the forest is its thickest and much of it is controlled by the lumber industry, second-, third-, and fourth-cut redwoods still swarm up and over ridges as far as you can see, the last diminished fragment of a sixty-million-year-old primeval forest that dominated much of North America, Europe, and Asia. As the logging of *Sequoia sempervirens* has played out over the last one hundred and fifty years, each successive cut has been of a tree even smaller than the one before, some impatiently logged off when not yet a foot thick, mere newborns in light of their species' genetic blueprint—the result a once-ancient forest now trapped in perpetual infancy.

Sempervirens are by design, of course, far grander than that.

When mature and well stocked with four-hundred-year-olds, redwood groves are typically canopied, casting the forest floor in perpetual shade and capturing an airy, cathedral emptiness between the bottom and the top. That enormous space—with patches of light filtering through its ceiling and drifting earthward like leaves on a stream—explains why a visit to an old-growth redwood grove, even in a park, is often considered a spiritual experience of the first order.

And I take no exception to that description. Indeed, I have come to love this tree. I have bonded with it, we have been through much together, and it has cast an inspirational shadow on the last half of my life. Our relationship turned into something far more profound than the usual human-to-plant interaction, with us eventually connecting, I believe, as just one being to another, without intermediation. My confessed communion with this tree seems anthropomorphic, I suppose, but it is no less real to me for seeming so. It is a story I have never revealed previously, intimidated by the potential disbelief of others and my own embarrassment, but I will tell this tale now: speaking without saying a word, *Sequoia sempervirens* reached out to me, saw me through much difficulty, and has hovered over my life like a totem right up to this day, often guiding me when I needed it most and teaching me much about myself that I might never have learned otherwise.

But it did not start out that way. Far from it.

I first met *Sequoia sempervirens* not as a fellow being or

even as a tree but as lumber sold by the board foot. Our introduction to each other took place behind my maternal grandparents' house on Fresno's McKenzie Avenue, in my Grandpa Jensen's rundown shop on the second floor over the storage room next to the garage that backed up on the alley. The '50s had just begun, my dad had just finished law school on the G.I. Bill, and I was on the verge of kindergarten. The workshop was lit by a single overhead bulb and was full of shadows, sawdust, and the smell of lubricating oil. Grandpa Jensen was a master woodworker at the Fresno Planing Mill and was missing part of a forefinger from an accident with a band saw when he was a young man. Over the years, he had accumulated pieces of wood he found "interesting," storing them in the rafters above his table saw and lathe. The redwood plank Grandpa revealed to me that first time was an inch thick, two feet wide, and eight feet long. Dust billowed throughout the shop as he fetched the plank and brushed it off. He made it very clear that this was no ordinary board he was showing me. He pointed out the grain and how tight and straight it was, how the growth rings pressed together, which meant it had been sawed from a very, very, very old tree. In my memory, the plank is scarlet and massive and I am small and awestruck by the scene. Grandpa claimed that he could leave that red board outside for the next twenty years and it would never rot. There was no wood like redwood, he told me. Orange light was leaking in the shop window, dust was still swirling. He also told me that there wouldn't be any boards left like that one when I got to be his age, and he turned out to be right.

I as yet, however, had no clue that *Sequoia sempervirens* would ever be more to me than just a special grade of lumber, much less that it would end up lodged so close to my heart.

WOOD GETS PERSONAL

As it has for all Northern Californians, redwood has been white noise in my life, always present in the background—so much so that it goes unaccounted for, just Muzak in our collective elevator.

Without us having to pay much if any attention to it, there is redwood everywhere here, even when there are no trees: we can buy a bag of Redwood Burgers from the Redwood Drive-In's drive-through window; fix our exhaust pipe at Redwood Muffler; acquire a second mortgage from the Redwood Credit Union; get down and dirty over cocktails at the Redwood Lounge; break the speed limit along the Redwood Highway; watch movies at the Redwood Theatre; graduate from Redwood High School or Redwood Middle School or Redwood Elementary School or Redwood Preschool, or even Redwood Daycare, not to mention College of the Redwoods; we can order linguini at the Redwood Café; mess around in the afternoon on the day rate at the Redwood Motel; buy potting soil from the Redwood Garden Center and Nursery; wash our cars at Redwood In-and-Out Car Wash; get our timepieces fixed at the Redwood Jewelry Emporium; fill our prescriptions at the Redwood Pharmacy; clean our drains with Redwood Roto-Rooter; and of course buy our redwood at Redwood Lumber.

The permutations have become endless: Redwood Dairy, Redwood Partners, Redwood Nursing Home, Redwood Construction, Redwood Used Cars, Redwood Cemetery, Redwood Veterinary Hospital, Redwood Answering Service, Redwood Roofing, Redwood Bicycle Shop, Redwood Video Rentals, Redwood Hair Salon, Redwood Steam Cleaning, and Redwood Etc., etc.

I moved from Fresno to the Bay Area, where redwoods are native, to attend a university whose mascot is a tree and whose logo is the profile of a *Sequoia sempervirens*, though it took me years to pay the silhouette of that tree much due. My daughter went to a high school that had a *sempervirens* on its logo as well. And we were just two of millions of Californians whose lives pass under a forest of such redwood shapes to this day.

By the time I was born, in 1946, the coast redwood had already provided an underpinning to the entire region. Literally. It was felled so San Francisco, Alameda, San Mateo, Santa Clara, Contra Costa, Marin, Sonoma, and Solano Counties could build and expand. Indeed, from the redwood's perspective, the Bay Area amounts to a massive *sempervirens* graveyard. I have been personally involved in remodeling three Bay Area houses over my lifetime, and each had been originally framed in studs cut from the same magnificent tight-grained ancient scarlet wood that my grandfather had treasured for me in his workshop, those boards nailed in place back in the days when such spectacular redwood seemed plentiful enough to be profligate within even the most common constructions, including forms for pouring concrete. This urban growth brought a Timber Rush to the Bay Area, fed at first by the nearby primeval forests and then, once all the easily available virgin first forest had been felled, reaching all the way to the Oregon border, where proximity to ancient dead redwood has become almost universal along the western slope of the Coast Range. Millions of Northern Californians are exposed to long-since-cut *Sequoia sempervirens* every day, and even if they don't know it, they are absorbing the species' energy—and even its perspective—through physical immersion, its chopped and sawed heartwood radiating behind our sheetrock and providing a seemingly everlasting presence.

Even so, few of us Californians notice, much less pursue, our connection to this tree any further than that. But I did. I took it a lot further. The truth is, out of the blue, it got personal for me, very personal, and things between myself and this species took on an intimate character that I would never have thought possible.

The precipitating event was my purchase of Number 841, the house I have lived in for the last thirty-four years. Stepping down a Marin County slope, just fifteen minutes by automobile from San Francisco, it is three miles as the crow flies from the Muir Woods National Monument and right next door to the Golden Gate National Recreation Area. Two of my new house's public rooms were lined with old-growth redwood, long since painted over, and most of its old walls were framed with the same. And, just a foot away from the right front corner of its roof, stood the trunk of the redwood that was about to become my companion in a sudden moment of epiphany, awakening me to the Presence of *sempervirens*, being to being, from then on out.

I named that redwood in front of my new home "Tree."

Judging by its size, I guess Tree had been growing for some thirty years when the original ranch house that became Number 841 was constructed on the slopes of Mount Tamalpais in 1932. By the time I bought 841 in 1984, Tree's trunk, now some 150 feet tall and seven feet thick at its base, was almost rubbing the front lip of the roof, a spacing no modern building department would ever have permitted, but now happily grandfathered in. Tree's branches hovered over three-quarters of the top floor, and the wired glass ceiling in the dining room allowed me to look right up its shaft to where the tip foreshortened into emptiness and swayed in the gusts blowing off the Pacific onto the foot of Coyote Ridge.

I was led to my connection with Tree by trust as well as proximity. You see, to live in Number 841, right next to this considerable redwood, was to be at Tree's mercy. Should for any reason Tree come down, even at such an immature size—from the redwood perspective—the house and most everything in it would be crushed. Nothing short of solid granite can deflect a *sempervirens* in the grip of gravity. Once I accepted that reality, it was only a small step further to make Tree seem a benign presence just for continuing to stand up straight. I took that approach with Tree immediately. It and I obviously had to be on the same side for both of our sakes.

I introduced myself to my new redwood while the movers were unloading their tractor trailer in the driveway. I had been packing boxes at our old house down the Peninsula for the last week, often twelve hours a day, and was already fried—I had put a dent in my new minivan, and my back felt like leftover trench warfare—and our moving day was only half done. Looking for a momentary respite, I ducked behind Tree, out of view. My wife Lacey and I had just mortgaged ourselves up to our eyebrows even though Number 841 was considered an "old white elephant": vacant for two years, with squirrels living in the dining room and a septic tank that leaked onto the hillside, not to mention the immense tree towering over it like a guillotine. The real estate agent didn't even want to show it to us, and the bank that owned it acted as if they were doing us a favor by even considering our bid. So by the time we completed four weeks of negotiations and reached moving day, I was feeling overrun and looking for an ally.

And in that moment I leaned on Tree, leading with the

crown of my head.

And right then I must have slipped through some spiritual portal into this redwood's force field, because I immediately felt a flow between us that carried my mind on the run straight into epiphany. I suppose it was a vision of sorts. This *sempervirens* was so big, with such incredible purchase on the earth, that it spoke to me and my need in a primal language of place. And, to my stunned surprise, I listened. The sensation resembled a hum, only it was silent, a three-dimensional vibration unlike anything I had ever experienced. It was accompanied by an abiding sense of safety. In that moment, Tree made me feel like I was connected all the way to the middle of the planet. Then I went into some kind of trance state in which my fatigue evaporated and I lost track of time. I felt reassured all over.

After perhaps three minutes, I stepped away from the redwood and receded back into the world of words, somewhat dazed but smiling like a crocodile. I felt like I had been welcomed, though I had no idea how what had just happened between myself and the tree had actually happened.

"Hey, Tree," I said.

Tree, however, made no more response, at least for the moment.

But that was the beginning between us.

From here on, I would search out Tree's hum at critical moments when I needed redwood mojo to help me cope, or understand, or both, and sometimes Tree would answer.

Which is why I'm so grateful still.

THE THEORY OF PRESENCE

While I obviously mean to make much of the extraordinary link that joined Tree and me, I don't mean to present my *sempervirens* as simply a large paranormal stick transmitting on an altogether different wavelength. Tree also played a rich and full role as a major participant in the ordinary daily life of our front yard: A rope swing was anchored to Tree's lowest branch, some twenty feet off the ground, and my children and their friends spent hours swinging back and forth, sometimes drifting sideways and fending off Tree's trunk with their feet, launching themselves into a spin. Two of our friends got married under Tree. Three times a year, I clipped off the four-foot bush of suckers that sprouted over and over out of a large knot at Tree's base, intent on intervening before any of those suckers could *sempervirens* their way into being a Tree themselves. That same cluster of fledgling would-be-tree redwood served as one of our favorite locations to hide Easter eggs. I hired a climber to thin out Tree's limbs to avoid the sail effect in high winds and regularly walked around Tree during the rainy season looking for cracks in the earth that might indicate instability, but I never found any. In the autumn, my redwood shed copious amounts of brown needles, in several waves, and I gathered them with my rake year after year, swearing amazement that any plant could produce so much for me to rake, which led to me imploring Tree to "lighten the fuck up." One year, I had to rebuild a chunk of the poured concrete front porch that Tree had knuckled with one of its roots. During a half dozen different winters, at least one of Tree's enormous limbs broke loose in the high wind and came tumbling, twice clipping the front corner of the roof and doing damage, and twice splintering the handrail on the stairs leading down to the garage. Falling limbs also took out a small stretch of fence running along the driveway.

Among Tree's lower branches, a host of nuthatches nests every year, sweeping down on our bird feeder in squadrons. There, they hang upside down and stuff themselves. Tree's higher branches also provide a roost for the juvenile red-tailed hawk that inevitably appears for a month in the late summer, making its first stop after being kicked out of its parental nest and forced to forage for itself. And Tree serves as a freeway for the gray and red squirrels accessing the roof. Raccoons have been spotted about halfway up on several occasions. Once a hive of wasps constructed a mud nest at the very tip of one of Tree's longest low limbs, terrorizing the front yard, and I had to hire a guy to drive up from Monterey to take down the nest. He walked out on Tree's limb until he got within range with a long stick, then dislodged the nest so it plunged through the air into a garbage can on the ground held by his assistant, who immediately clapped a lid on the can so none of the furious wasps could escape.

Tree would have been a member of my family had there been nothing but these homespun encounters between us. But, of course, there was much more, and it was out of the ordinary, to say the least.

Looking back on my accumulated years of fragmentary communion with Tree—a moment here and a moment there, me always wondering what was going on while the incidents transpired, looking for the redwood to elevate me over the hurdle I was facing—I have developed a theory about what made our relationship possible: It seems to me that Presence, the energy pattern that living things displace in the way they occupy their space, is itself a language capable of communication with another Presence, despite existing in, in effect, a separate dimension in which words themselves had no immediate traction. Such an interchange is conditional on both Presences being awake to the moment and occupying the same present tense, witness to both themselves and the other—all internal energy channeled to their respective corporeal postures and their mutual intersection, Thought turned off, Being to the max. My exhaustion had put me in just such an available posture when Tree and I first engaged, and over the years that followed, I learned by trial and error that my distress seemed to trigger the flow of vibration between me and my tree. In such a state, I was often hurt and lost to the point that I was more present than ever, events having crowded me into a closet of pain or despair, contracting my focus to only the most immediate sensations, excluding past or future through total immersion in the Now, by force of circumstance if not spiritual mastery. As I observed it, Tree seemed to have little interest in the small shit of my life and ignored such situations wholesale. But when big and trying times arrived on my doorstep and I brought them to it, Tree was ready to engage them, and me. Afterward, I would search out words into which to translate the hum for memory's sake.

In those encounters with Tree, I usually stood close by Tree's trunk, closing my eyes and locating its Presence in the air that drifted across my shoulders. When I finally sensed that the redwood was There with a capital T, I touched the trunk and, if it was to be, the hum of *sempervirens* energy would jump down my arm and into my heart, shaped and targeted to the dilemma plaguing me, a message to be experienced rather than described or evoked.

When my dog, Fat Albert, died, old and sick, my first loss since moving to Number 841, Tree's hum carried me back to Albert's younger days, when he had ruled our block down the Peninsula. Then Tree revealed a mental path to an Albert who still lived on inside me and would never disappear until I did. The encounter lasted only a minute but seemed timeless. And I felt whole and full of Albert after it was over.

When my health collapsed following a six-month run of working sixteen-hour days, seven days a week, in order to meet a publisher's deadline, then instantly followed by three more grueling months starting up another project and commuting back and forth to New York, I finally threw myself at the foot of Tree. Some days, I barely had the strength to stand, but the doctors I consulted could find no obvious physical reason for my weakness. When I curled up against the redwood, my eyes closed, I felt as though I was being cradled and rocked as soon as I touched its bark, and my weakness immediately devolved into a wave of complete helplessness. Then the hum amplified and I could no longer distinguish myself from Tree's mighty purchase on the earth beneath me, and a current of strength flowed out of the ground, carried on the hum, and into my belly. My body absorbed it like a dry sponge. And while that was going on, I was reminded of my own resourcefulness. I found myself in the dirt under Tree fifteen minutes after I had started. Two weeks later, I had recouped the physical wherewithal to return to work.

Tree was also there for the worst moment of my professional career. After traveling back and forth to New York over three years, working as the authorized biographer of a Manhattan media tycoon and almost burning myself out in the process, the whole arrangement came a cropper when the tycoon's lawyers killed my project. I was devastated at having been used as shabbily as I had, and for weeks I refused to be consoled, to the point of being a genuine pain in the ass to everyone who came in contact with me, myself included. I spent weeks hunkered down in my office, feeling very sorry for myself and grinding my teeth. When I finally turned to Tree, the *sempervirens* hummed open my clenched hands and allowed me to exhale. I stood for almost an hour at its base, my eyes closed, slowly realizing that if I didn't separate myself from my anger and dial back my self-pity, I would blow up my life and my family out of sheer petulance. With that, I felt myself tumbling head over heels until Tree's hum snatched me out of the air. From there on, the *sempervirens* just soothed me over and over, like a hand petting a cat. And at the end of the hour, I felt released from my hurt. Tree's hum seemed to have suctioned all the bile out of me.

A year later, I was back to Tree as I tried to quit smoking after twenty-five years as a three-pack-a-day tobacco addict. For two weeks running, as my system struggled to detoxify, I started each day by taking to the *sempervirens* in the front yard the morning tremors that made me rattle like an old truck on a bad road. I would touch with my open palms, trying to remain still, sensing calm flowing my way against much resistance, and feeling the urge to suck smoke into my lungs dissipate sufficiently to proceed with the rest of my day. I have never lit up a cigarette since.

My special connection to Tree was confirmed forever three years after that, in the immediate aftermath of the greatest loss of my life. I spent the last two of those years nursing my wife

Lacey through a painful struggle with breast cancer that ended with her in Intensive Care, on a breathing machine, and me petitioning to have her removed so she could die on her own terms. As prescribed for Buddhists, her body was laid out in our front room, some ten yards from Tree, and then cremated. The day after, I walked out to Tree. For the previous two years, I had never allowed myself to face up to my helplessness in the situation, a way of clinging to the notion that I was supposed to save her and could somehow find a way to do so by trying even harder than I already had. I dropped into an emotional free fall now that no such rescue was possible. I felt more empty and spent than I had ever felt. But I could never bring myself to cry. Then, at last, I pressed my body against Tree, chest to bark, and grabbed it with my arms spread in a hug. And it was as if a door had blown open in a stiff breeze. Tears gushed where before none would. Sobs engulfed me and I was sure Tree must have been crying too.

SEVEN REDWOOD VIRTUES

I have to admit that my strange companionship with Tree not only opened my heart and transformed my perspective of the species *Sequoia sempervirens* but also changed how I viewed my own *Homo sapiens* species as well. Indeed, I have come to realize that this very, very large plant—depicted on postcards, embossed on ashtrays, and commonly used by humans to construct patio decks and garden planters—is in truth a repository of virtues not only essential to *sempervirens* but necessary to the rejuvenation and eventual survival of modern humanity as well. There is much we need to know that *sempervirens* might teach us. That is a lot to lay off on a tree, even one so very large, but consider the species as a role model:

Redwoods take very good care of themselves. Indeed, self-reliance is embedded in the *sempervirens* gene pool. Its red flesh is resistant to insects, fungal infections, and rot. Its outer bark, sometimes more than a foot thick, is a fire inhibitor. It has adapted to the resource of drippy coastal fog by growing water receptors in its foliage, enabling it to nourish itself not just through its roots but through its crown as well. It controls its birth rate by generating a toxicity in the ground around it that limits the fertility of the seeds it spews out in tiny cones. Left alone, *Sequoia sempervirens* is a very efficient, self-contained organism for propagating life as it has known it. In contrast, *Homo sapiens*, rather than self-nurturing, is instead dependent on a steadily expanding social and commercial infrastructure to survive; we are often emotionally helpless when stripped of our technological exoskeletons, and our sustainability without the intervention of elaborate external apparatuses is suspect at best. This, of course, bodes serious ill for *Homo sapiens* as our complex systems begin to crumble under the weight of our accumulated carbon exhaust. We always need something else to give us a leg up and cover our blind spots lest we unravel. That may be unavoidable, at least to a degree, but such dependency on Stuff is also debilitating and stands out as the proverbial canary in the mineshaft of human existence. And it offers us a good reason to act more like a tree, odd as that may seem.

Redwood is quiet. Human life is increasingly framed in clatter and cacophony at every turn, generating disorientation, delusion, and discord. Our noise never ceases. It amps up the speed of everything it touches and contributes mightily to our failure to listen to each other or to ourselves, thereby diminishing both our intellectual understanding and our spiritual grasp. It ensures that we are, in effect, never alone and never still. And without the experience of being alone and still, we short ourselves of insight, self-knowledge, and, ultimately, wisdom. A grove of *sempervirens*, however, is still and soundless, Quiet writ large, so silent that it amounts to its own kind of loud. Standing motionless under a redwood canopy, I found the quiet tangible, as though I could reach out and shake its hand. The virtue in that experience is apparent to those who have had it. Such quiet throws us back on our own inner workings, the first step toward learning who we are or who we need to be, or both.

Redwood is long term. As a species, modern *Homo sapiens* has trouble thinking beyond the remainder of the day, much less into the next week; we are short term. Our attention spans are shorter still, ruled by the immediate gratification of text messages, instant mashed potatoes, and galvanic response that leave us living in the Now in the most narrow and debilitating version of such a posture. The thought of planning or acting over the horizon in the interest of generations yet to come is largely political and social anathema. And that contortion may very well prove our undoing. Not surprisingly, the result of such truncated vision is a legacy of Shortsightedness, Thoughtless Consumption, and Institutionalized Selfishness, eventually to be overrun by Bills Come Due and Chickens Come Home to Roost. *Sempervirens*, however, operates in cycles hundreds of years long. Its today is derived from centuries of yesterdays and projected into centuries of tomorrows. Typically, the coast redwood acts in pursuit of outcomes in the next millennia as a matter of course. Its clock has no second hand, or minute hand either. It flows with time rather than conquering, consuming, and then disposing of it hour by hour. There are no transients in a redwood grove; every tree is in it for the long haul. Yet among *Homo sapiens*, everyone seems to be just passing through, with allegiance to the immediate moment and only the immediate moment.

Redwood is a community. From a human-design standpoint, questions are sometimes raised about the *sempervirens*'s root system because it lacks a deep taproot to support its enormous height. Indeed, its roots are shallow and widespread, a "deficiency" for which it compensates with mutual assistance. Its shallow roots reach out to wrap around and join with those of the surrounding trees, creating a network of shared strength and stability to empower each and all to resist the leverage of winds that might otherwise pose a mortal threat. We *sapiens*, on the other hand, have pursued an obsession with singularity and individualism to a point that our obsession often denies us access to the mutuality that is a critical, if often ignored or defiled, ingredient in the human possibility. Without such community, we suffer through loneliness, abandonment, hopelessness, and anomie, for which the only antidote is access to each other. We also separate our fates and eliminate our pooling of resources so that we are always afflicted with haves and have-nots, as well as with the nightmare of scarcity. There are circumstances in which togetherness and sharing are required above all else and, having nurtured privatization to the exclusion of tenancy in common, we find ourselves ill equipped to realize that aspect of our humanity when we need it most. Compassion is our highest human calling, but we cannot pursue it without membership in a larger circle, and so, by default, we end up trapped in our lesser selves.

Redwood is patient. Sometimes positive outcomes require us to simply wait. Yet tolerance of such waiting has become a casualty in the pace of modern civilization and *sapiens'* growing insistence on forcing the issue rather than allowing it to ripen into the opportune. We are in a constant hurry, anxious to get on to whatever is supposed to be next, occupying a mental space only a half step short of panic when faced with inaction or stymied in our pursuit of seemingly forward motion, epitomized by our road rage at the traffic jam, always inclined to drop what we are doing and try a different approach on the promise of immediate resolution, no matter how flimsy. *Sempervirens*, on the other hand, waits. In a redwood grove, where among the cluster of trees each struggles to find a patch of sunlight under the canopy, a young tree may spend decades the size of a seedling until an old tree nearby dies and topples, at last leaving a sunny open space overhead for the patient seedling to fill, the potential of growth now available to it in the nurturing light, its time having finally arrived. It often seems to me that a strong dose of such patience would cure half our modern ills.

Redwood knows where it came from. Under a *Sequoia sempervirens* canopy, the air is heavy with the time that preceded, and I feel the years in that air on my skin like I feel the weather, our planetary timeline present at every turn. Not only are many of the trees ancient in their own right, but the species itself provides a long genetic pathway back through centuries to a common memory of which we can partake in its company. Under *sempervirens*'s shadow, I feel membership in the accumulation of time and experience that is the underpinning of wisdom, digesting what brought us so far and identifying the dead ends and shortfalls discarded along the way. Meanwhile, our human history, subject to the limits of our own consciousness, is increasingly obscured by our disinterest, narcissism, ignorance, and shriveled attention span. Indeed, most modernized *sapiens* have lost track of events more than a decade behind us, effectively orphaned from themselves and their ancestry. We cannot learn because we are so busy forgetting. Who we are is not just a manufacture of the moment, it is an inheritance that needs to be embraced or lost. And it seems we have chosen to lose it, having convinced ourselves that we somehow started with a blank slate. Like all species, however, we start where those before us left off, even if we pretend otherwise.

Redwood is calm. This is the redwood's companion virtue to Quiet. Under the *sempervirens* canopy there is none of the seething energy and incessant activity associated with tropical rainforests, full of birds and monkeys and rodents of every description in perpetual motion. Redwood groves, on the other hand, are flat water. A few sea birds leave the canopy in the morning and return as the sun sets, but otherwise the old-growth redwood forest feels unoccupied, undisturbed, and largely devoid of internal pressure. To those experiencing it, it seems a world at rest. This, again, stands in marked contrast to the world of *Homo sapiens*, where hysteria and modernity quite often go hand in hand. In our human world, anxiety has become a constant, along with obsession, fixation, tension, and the delusion that accompanies all things hyper. Everything and everyone is unsettled and becoming more so. Worry is ubiquitous, and we're all hooked on the internal uneasiness that threatens everything with disturbance and disruption. In the human world, calm is ordinarily noticeable only in its absence—except under the redwood canopy, where frantic is forever out of place and equanimity is broadcast from tree to tree to tree. Without it, we are working overtime and driving ourselves crazy at every opportunity.

THE REDWOOD MASSACRE

In addition to experiencing *Sequoia sempervirens* as a spiritual and emotional resource, I have also come to identify it as a victim that endured an incalculable loss at the hands of *Homo sapiens*—indeed, a holocaust from the redwood perspective—in which the entire species was targeted in a one-sided war and forced to run a gauntlet of misery over the course of a century and a half in which its historic identity was culled almost to its vanishing point. In 1850, just before the assault on the ancient redwood forest began in earnest, California was host to more than two million acres of full-fledged old-growth primeval *sempervirens* forest, groves dotted with hundred-year-old juveniles, four-hundred-year-old adults, and thousand-year-old elders grouped around an inner cathedral catacomb, direct descendants in a line of trees that had never been cut or sawed or felled in sixty million years, their woodland floor instead littered with gigantic fallen trunks, dead of old age, who had sprouted around the time the New Testament was being written, or even earlier. Then commenced some hundred and fifty years of cutting, sawing, and felling old-growth coast redwood following the discovery of gold in the Sacramento watershed and California's almost immediate induction as the thirty-first state in the union. And after those hundred and fifty years, a little more than a hundred thousand acres of virgin forest remained, divided among scattered patches around the North Coast, under the protection of the state and federal governments, and sheltered by the insistent concern of generations of Good Samaritans intent on saving the species from extinction.

Looking over Tree's proverbial shoulder at those hundred and fifty years, it now appears to have been a massacre of epic proportions, despite the efforts to stop it.

Typically, this scourge's arrival in an old-growth *Sequoia sempervirens* grove took form as a crew of a dozen or so men, invading early in the new year to set up camp nearby and begin assessing where to start dealing out the premature death and dismemberment that was, from the redwood perspective, the *Homo sapiens* calling card. The initial crew would be followed by three or four dozen more *sapiens* as their attack progressed into the spring and summer. Redwoods had to be felled one by one, and felling was a challenging technique. If a falling *sempervirens* crashed to the ground with the wrong distribution of weight, the corpse would shatter and instantly lose most of its monetary value, so a landing bed was prepared along an unobstructed avenue to soften the impact. It was the job of the "choppers" to make sure the doomed tree fell where it was supposed to, with its worth intact. Working with razor-sharp double-headed axes mounted on handles almost four feet long, the choppers first constructed a platform that allowed them to cut into the redwood about six feet above ground level. They then carved out a wedge-shaped "undercut," a slice whose mouth was tall enough for an adult to stand up in. The undercut extended to the tree's central core and would eventually control the direction of the *sempervirens*'s dying collapse. That accomplished, the "sawyers" went to work slightly higher on the opposite side of the wounded redwood's trunk, using a twelve-foot saw pushed and pulled by *sapiens* at each end. As their cut advanced, steel wedges were driven into the breach in the redwood's trunk. Those wedges eventually provided the leverage necessary to topple the mortally wounded tree along the trajectory laid out by the undercut. That toppling into redwood death could be heard all over the surrounding hillside: a "whoosh" as it fell, displacing so much air that it sucked the crew's breath right out of their lungs, followed by a thunderous concussion and shock wave that shook the earth under their feet.

Once that fresh *sempervirens* corpse was brought to ground, the "peelers" set to work stripping off its bark and limbs using saws and long pointed bars. Then the sawyers went back at it, this time wielding a one-man eight-foot saw to divide the twenty-foot-thick dead trunk into logs somewhere between twelve and twenty feet long. In the meantime, the *sapiens* attackers had constructed a skid road, composed of foot-thick logs corduroyed into the earth. Each enormous dismembered segment of the dead redwood would be dragged out of the grove on that skid road by a team of eight to twelve oxen, driven by the "bull puncher" with the assistance of a "water packer" and a "chain tender." If the enormous section of dead redwood moved too slowly, it would hang up and require a crew to leverage it back into motion using hand tools and a winch. If it moved too fast, it would run over the oxen towing it, and their bull puncher. The skid road ended at a landing next to a spur railroad, where the remains of the once two-hundred-foot-tall *sempervirens* were leveraged onto railroad cars, one log per car. The spur line brought those remains to a mill pond where they were floated, waiting for their turn to be run through the massive saws that were the final step necessary to turn an ancient living tree into a very tall stack of dead boards, laid out in a drying yard before shipment to construction projects all over the state, each board some fifteen or twenty times older than California itself.

Back at the grove where the massacre had started, the ground was awash in sun for the first time in millennia. Ferns and sorrel were shriveling in the hot light. Fragments of dead trees were strewn across the landscape—a limb here, a strip of bark there. The inner cathedral had vanished into thin air. The only trees left standing were those too small to be worth killing. And stumps? Everywhere, and soon to be covered in sprouts as the decapitated roots of thousand-year-old giants began patiently trying to regenerate what they had once been.

This pattern of extermination was repeated tens of thousands of times over the holocaust years, up and down the Coast Range, along the watersheds of the Eel, the Navarro, the Russian, the Mattole, the Mad, and the Smith Rivers, the region relentlessly updated with steam engines, tractors, and chain saws along the way. Thanks to the citizen advocacy led by Save the Redwoods League, in the 1920s the first parks were created to give refuge to surviving old-growth *Sequoia sempervirens*, but the process was slow and arduous and terribly incomplete.

And then the old-growth redwood holocaust was over. The meager 5 percent of old-growth *sempervirens* that was going to be saved had been; all 95 percent of old-growth *sempervirens* that was going to be executed and dismembered had been as well. And we are left—lining up at Muir Woods, Redwood Creek, Rockefeller Forest, and the Avenue of the Giants—to try to recognize and account for that which is now irretrievably diminished or lost to us, to our children, to their children, and to all the children from here on, or for at least a thousand years, if *Homo sapiens* makes it that far. We inherited an astonishing artifact, unique and delicately crafted by the life force that turned this planet into our home, and we proceeded to trash it in the name of building materials.

Shame on us.

THE LAST STAND

I witnessed the final episode in that *Homo sapiens* assault on the coast redwood's original forest. And driven by the fruits of my own professional investigation and my eventual reporter's indignation at how this final showdown had come to pass, I ended up outraged by this last chapter as well—not just because of my relationship with Tree but particularly by how much the end was dominated by *sapiens*'s lesser self. And when it was over, I was also overrun with a new reverence for that which remained.

By 1989, the only significant concentration of old-growth *sempervirens* whose fate still hung in the balance between parkland and lumber was some seventy-five hundred contiguous acres owned by the Pacific Lumber Company in Humboldt County at the headwaters of Salmon Creek and the Elk River, four miles northwest of the town of Fortuna and eight miles south of the city of Eureka, on the western slope that sweeps down to Humboldt Bay and the mouth of the Eel. When the spotlight eventually fell on this last stand, it would be referred to as the Headwaters Forest, and for several years it would become the most notorious and newsworthy forest in the state. Its fate started getting personal for me after I emerged from the haze following my collapsed project with the media tycoon—assisted out of my funk by Tree, as you will recall— and I convinced my publisher to underwrite a book about the struggle that broke out on the North Coast when the Pacific Lumber Company and its last old-growth *sempervirens* came into play. I eventually spent the next six years—including a two-year break to nurse Lacey—driving back and forth to Humboldt County, staying in a twenty-five-dollar-a-night motel on Highway 101, interviewing some fifty participants and reviewing reams of court documents and depositions in order to portray "the struggle between Wall Street and Main Street over California's ancient redwoods." I told my publisher that the book would chronicle how *Homo sapiens* decided what to do with the last virgin outpost of California's signature species. And the book did so, in spades.

The Pacific Lumber Company—known around Humboldt as PL—had old growth remaining when none of the other timber companies in California did because PL had husbanded its ancient forest while the other corporations massacred theirs in the interest of short-term profits. Indeed, by the 1980s, PL's Mill B, in the company town of Scotia, upstream from the Eel delta, housed the one remaining saw rig in the state big enough to handle elder virgin *sempervirens* logs. PL's foresters calculated how many board feet had to be harvested each year to match the forest's estimated annual growth and never let the former exceed the latter, showing singular restraint in an industry notorious for cutting with abandon at breakneck pace. By PL's calculations, its maverick rate of harvest left it with enough old growth to allow PL's choppers and sawyers to assault virgin *sempervirens* forest at that same rate until 2045. That "slow" cut, however, cast the company as an "underperformer" on Wall Street, and by 1985, the Street's financial sharks, armed with junk bonds, were on the hunt for companies like PL, which not only had cornered the market in a valuable resource but also had no debt to speak of.

That caught the attention of one Charles Hurwitz, a Texas-based "corporate takeover artist," who secretly purchased control of PL using money borrowed with the assistance of junk-bond king Michael Milken, before Milken was convicted of securities fraud and sent to prison. At Hurwitz's first appearance in Humboldt County after his purchase, he addressed the company's workforce and reassured them that despite all the scary rumors they might have heard about him, he believed in the Golden Rule as it is apparently practiced in the state of Texas: "Those who have the gold rule." His audience laughed nervously. Hurwitz then began remaking Pacific Lumber according to his own financial imperatives. He liquidated the employee retirement fund, sold off PL's ancillary companies, and "upstreamed" all the proceeds to his Texas parent corporation. In the forest, he tripled PL's rate of cut, finishing off isolated stands of old growth and clear-cutting the company's sizeable inventory of very large second growth as though there were not a minute to lose, again upstreaming the considerable proceeds back to Texas. Then he turned his corporate gaze on the Headwaters Forest, and the final battle over primeval California was joined.

Hurwitz had faced opposition since his raid on PL stock first became known; dissent included lawsuits from PL stockholders, complaints from local residents, suits over the erosion resulting from the company's logging practices, and political and media campaigns by environmental activists. That opposition became statewide when he dispatched cutters and sawyers into the Headwaters. There, Hurwitz's plans were challenged under California's belated forestry statutes and timbering permit process, and he was eventually held at bay when the courts invoked the Endangered Species Act to delay most of his Headwaters logging plans. That stalemate lasted until 1999, when California's senior United States senator cut a deal with the Texas raider. According to its terms, the state and federal governments purchased the entire Headwaters Forest for some $460 million—all quickly upstreamed—and those old-growth groves at the origin of Salmon Creek and the Elk River joined *Sequoia sempervirens*'s surviving 5 percent. Hurwitz also agreed to cut none of the remaining tiny pockets of old growth on PL's other lands and, shortly thereafter, the gargantuan Mill B and its old-growth saws were dismantled, now too big to be of any practical use.

In 2007, the Pacific Lumber Company—out of old growth, having used up much of its second- and third-growth forest in Charles Hurwitz's logging frenzy, and then spun off into a separate freestanding corporate entity—filed for bankruptcy relief from its bondholders. The company that had once been debt free now had more than $1 billion in unpayable liabilities, and bankruptcy court would soon auction off its remaining assets, including the company town of Scotia and whatever additional items of worth had not yet been forwarded on to Texas. According to court documents, Charles Hurwitz walked away with more than $3 billion of the company's value, all of which had long since been parked beyond the reach of PL's creditors.

Shame on him.

SNEAKING INTO THE PRIMEVAL

Before the Headwaters Forest had been rescued from Charles Hurwitz, I visited it on the sly. And that visit pretty much closed the circle on the devotion to *Sequoia sempervirens* that had first been kindled in me by Tree and has since become such a significant, if heretofore hidden, feature in my personal cosmology.

The Headwaters Forest was still private property, trespassing forbidden, and I had already been denied official permission to enter it by PL's local manager. But as a reporter, I felt I needed to at least eyeball this grove in order to really understand the story I was collecting. So I contacted Greg, one of the environmental activists leading the fight to stop PL, and took him up on his offer to smuggle me in. Greg was under a court injunction to stay off PL's lands, but he was game to guide me nonetheless. I also brought along my then twenty-five-year-old son, Gabe, and Cheri, the woman I would eventually marry. There was active logging going on right next to our old-growth destination, so the plan was to wait for Friday night after the PL crew had left the site and the sun was down, then hike in on the logging road, hide in the old growth until Sunday evening, and then sneak back out under the cover of darkness, leaving no one the wiser when PL's crew returned Monday morning.

Cheri and I rendezvoused with Greg and Gabe around 9 p.m. at the home of another environmental activist in Fortuna, where we left our cars. Our host then dropped the four of us at the locked gate to the logging road. We hopped over it and took off, each carrying about twenty-five pounds in our backpacks. The hike was some twelve miles with a gain of eighteen hundred feet in elevation, passing through the dark shadows of the second-growth forest as we climbed, pushing the pace like a pack of burglars, which, technically, we were. Everyone was gassed by 2 a.m., when we reached an open spot off the road and Greg announced we had arrived. For secrecy's sake, no one turned on a flashlight as we laid out in our sleeping bags. After dozing fitfully, we would enter the Headwaters at the first light of day.

It was only then that I realized we had been sleeping in a clear-cut. The area was dotted with fresh redwood stumps, and slash from the logging was all over the otherwise bald ground. The sap was pungent, laced with the smell of chain saws. Insects swarmed the debris. The scene was as ugly as ugly could be, complete with a couple of discarded Coca-Cola cans. We got moving again right away and crossed the cut, took a hard left downhill, where the ugliest ugly ended, and plunged into the Headwaters Forest. Within ten more steps we had entered another dimension, one of perpetual shade and half-light, green and more green, and the softest air I have ever breathed.

Though I hadn't anticipated it, my entry was a step through another spiritual portal, like that first time with Tree, only now the silent hum was at an order of magnitude beyond what I had ever experienced before, the envelopment total and immediate, with more Presence going down than you could shake a stick at, even if it wasn't much of a picture-postcard place. The Headwaters Forest did not look like the more famous redwood refuges down on the rich alluvial flats; much of the Headwaters was sloped and scruffy, littered with its own discards. But I was transported by it anyway. A working-man's cathedral lived on under the canopy. Dead wood cluttered the view upward, with many trees wedged against each other; it was not much in the way of majestic, but it was long on earnestness and tenacity as it somehow managed to feel holy from the inside out.

At first, we pushed through a thicket of four-foot-tall salal bushes, with their leathery leaves and occasional bunches of inedible red berries. Then we entered a stretch of fallen *sempervirens* elders. Twelve- and twenty-foot-thick redwood trunks had toppled in profusion over centuries and were layered one atop another atop another, in a waffle pattern, the lowest layer the most deteriorated. The only way through was to climb to the top and walk along the highest trunk, which looked to have been seeded about the time the Normans invaded England. The one underneath it may very well have dated from when Mohammad conquered Mecca. When the one beneath that was still a seedling, Carthage was a world power. And standing on top of them all, absorbing Presence from each, I felt like I was elevated on the tip of time itself, going back as far as back goes. I lingered there for a while, drawing power from what had once been, feeling the hum rising through my feet.

Eventually we left the waffle and found our way to a flat where the canopy was a little thinner and sunlight flickered like confetti. Two-foot-high sorrel covered the ground, and every seat on it was soft. We made that clearing our basecamp. It was marked by a young tree, perhaps a hundred feet tall. This *sempervirens* had spent its life chasing light, growing upward in a corkscrew, and was an easy landmark to locate. From there, we explored, following a creek bed for a while, heading downslope, then circling around and returning to the corkscrew tree as the light began to fade and the silence was broken by a flock of marbled murrelets returning to their nests in the canopy, having spent their day chasing fish in the Pacific Ocean.

That night I dreamt I was lying in sorrel three times as deep as the cover I was actually in. I seemed to be hiding, with great trepidation, yoked with the weight of grief I had woken to every morning since Lacey's death. Then, in full dream mode, I suddenly sprang to my feet and lifted up in the air, sailing along underneath the canopy. The weight I had been carrying was replaced with a lightness of being that powered my flying about through the treetops, though I had no idea how it did so. I looked down and I saw myself balanced on the waffle, then again sprawled in the sorrel, feeling a hum that was wound to its top-end r.p.m. and that lifted off both scenes like heat off a griddle. Then, as I swooped around, I woke halfway and found myself on the real ground. I looked up and could barely discern the corkscrew against a more-than-charcoal sky. I was momentarily convinced the twisted tree was watching me. Then I tumbled back into sleep, woke the next morning without that weight for the first time in months, and spent the day exploring some more.

The most impressive trait the Headwaters Forest brought to the table was its wildness. From every angle, it was savage and untamed. There were no tracks to follow through this old growth besides the ones we had made ourselves. Indeed, these seventy-five hundred acres had been the last to be scheduled for cutting because they were an out-of-the-way, cluttered tangle, all uphill and downhill that would be a challenge to scalp.

Even so, the vigor of this final survivor defied its unprepossessing veneer. It was truly uncontrolled and untrammeled, a place where every time we touched something, it seemed to be the first touch of it ever. When Sunday night arrived, I felt renewed and enlarged by this forest's stubborn grip on life and grateful that such a place might be saved, even if no one ever visited it. The hum it generated followed me into the clear-cut for a bit on our hike out.

We were met at the locked gate just before midnight on Sunday and taken to fetch our cars. When I got home to Number 841 the next day, I went straight to Tree, still inspired and lightened and thinking I could somehow share what I had been through and the boost it had given me. But Tree showed no sign of recognition, not saying anything one way or another.

SAVE THE REDWOOD, SAVE THE HUMAN

This is not to say that there was any breakdown between Tree and me. We continue as boon, if occasional, companions to this day. Cheri and I got married next to Tree. Tree provided solace when my mother died and comfort through my dog Pancho's end, and then my dog Tyrone's. It gave me something to hold on to while under fire from some serious PTSD. There were also several best friends whose deaths Tree bolstered me through, as well as the approaching deaths of several more, not to mention the withering of my career. And these days I spend a lot of time leaning against its trunk considering my own death as well.

Choosing to confess what has gone on between the coast redwood and myself was a big decision, but Tree wasn't involved in making it. Tree only came to me in my misery, and this story has made me anything but miserable. Tree taught me to see at least a few things through another species' eyes, and that turns out to have been a liberation and an empowerment. I confess and explain my feelings now because I am an old man and want to make myself clear while I still can.

Homo sapiens has done serious, potentially fatal, damage to the planet's capacity to sustain life as we have known it. And now we have reached a moment when we must drastically change our behavior or collapse. For the first time in ten thousand years, and thanks to our own actions, *Homo sapiens* is about to be in as much danger as all the rest of the species around us have previously been at our hands. And the path to our own species' rescue and redemption going forward has already been marked by the Good Samaritans who saved what they could among these surrounding species in years past. Now all of us must do likewise: nurturing, husbanding, and protecting all those other beings—animal, vegetable, mineral—who have managed to make it this far. We save ourselves by saving them; we prosper when they prosper; their ongoing diminishment diminishes us; their elevation is our uplift; and we can only make ourselves whole by insisting that they be included in our reconstruction.

The time has come for all forms of life to make common cause.

So *sempervirens* and I went ahead and did just that.

DAVID HARRIS *is a former contributing editor at* Rolling Stone *and the* New York Times Magazine *and is the author of eleven books. His book* The Last Stand, *which chronicles the fate of the Pacific Lumber Company, was reissued by Heyday in 2018.*

Guardians of the Giants
Gary Ferguson

ONE HUNDRED YEARS OF SAVE THE REDWOODS LEAGUE

On August 2, 1919, the Garden Court at San Francisco's regal Palace Hotel was, as usual, thick with the hum and bustle of California's movers and shakers—politicians and bankers and business tycoons and entertainers. Hands fluttered under shimmering glass pendant chandeliers, while waiters moved in and out from between the marble columns at the edges of the room in a scene that seemed to anticipate F. Scott Fitzgerald's *Great Gatsby* years before Gatsby himself hit the page. Many of the patrons were letting out sighs of relief over the recently signed Treaty of Versailles, delivering a merciful end to World War I—a treaty President Wilson had stumped for the previous spring at a luncheon right here at the Garden Court. Others talked excitedly about how, the month before, a British dirigible had become the first airship to cross the Atlantic. And at least a few at the Garden Court that day were likely running their fingers up and down their glasses of Scotch or vermouth—or even that new drink, the "1919"—looking wistful, wondering how their social lives might change come January, when prohibition would become the law of the land.

But for seven eager-looking men huddled together at one particular table—four University of California professors, an oil magnate, a New York aristocrat, and the effervescent, charismatic director of the National Park Service—there was something else on their minds, something they believed was of utmost urgency. It had to do with the troubling fact that with every passing week more of the state's magnificent redwood trees—which naturalist John Muir once described in the *New York Times* as "the glory of the Coast Range . . . [surpassing] in massive, sustained grandeur . . . all the other timber woods of the world"—were falling with unprecedented speed to the lumbermen's saws. In March of 1918, three of the men at that table had created a preservation group called Save the Redwoods League. Now, with demand for redwood after the end of the war driving a frenzy of cutting, it was time to form a board of directors and get down to business. Little did they know they were laying the foundation for what would soon grow into one of the most influential conservation groups of the century.

Logging redwoods was nothing new. In fact, lumbering

operations along the coast proper had started decades earlier, way back in 1850, when big trees were being sawed down and hauled off by ship from Humboldt Bay. It would take only about twenty years to empty the coast of nearly all of its magnificent redwoods. By the turn of the century, the harder-to-reach interior portions of the inland redwood empire had fallen under control of a handful of large timber companies, none of whom wasted any time establishing new mills and railroad lines and sprawling camps in the woods to house their workers. The axes and crosscut saws (often called "misery whips") of the late nineteenth century would be replaced by steam-powered drag saws and then gasoline-fueled chain saws. Whereas in the mid-1800s logs were carried out of the woods with teams of oxen and horses, or else floated on large rafts of logs down nearby rivers, animal power would soon yield to so-called steam donkeys, invented by a timber man from Eureka, which pulled the logs from where they fell to places where they could be loaded onto rail cars and carried to the mills. In a nutshell, thanks to massive doses of money and powerful new industrial technologies, the mighty redwoods were falling more easily than ever before.

As is true of most products, the demand for redwood lumber ebbed and flowed. It exploded following the devastating San Francisco earthquake of 1906; indeed many of the new buildings erected in the wake of that tragedy were constructed almost entirely of redwood. And around the time of that first

Save the Redwoods League board meeting at the Palace Hotel, amidst an intensifying postwar development boom, the annual cut had swelled to more than 520 million board feet annually—enough to fill a line of modern logging trucks stretched bumper to bumper from San Francisco nearly to Omaha.

The genesis of the idea to form Save the Redwoods League had sparked during a road trip. In the summer of 1917, three of the men at that Palace Hotel board meeting—Madison Grant, Henry Fairfield Osborn, and John C. Merriam—had traveled north out of San Francisco in search of what had by then become a somewhat fabled stand of redwoods. They stood in a flat at the base of Grasshopper Mountain, beside beautiful Bull Creek, which poured east past the silent groves in a sweet tumble of clear water, making for the South Fork of the Eel River.

To their enormous delight, the Bull Creek redwoods lived up to their reputation. More than a hundred of the big trees there towered over three hundred feet tall, the heart of a forest that no less than John Muir considered to be among the finest groves of redwoods in the state. Parking their car, Merriam, Osborn, and Grant walked through the grove in a hush, awestruck by the slant of afternoon light pouring through the giant trees, every step they took muffled by thick cushions of needles. They felt as if they were passing through some kind of spectacular ancient cathedral.

Yet for all the thrill they felt during that visit, almost from the time they stepped from their car, the sturdy, timeless magnificence of the place seemed precarious, steadily weakened by the chug and rumble of nearby logging operations. In fact, the relentless commotion of the cutting was coming ever closer to that great cathedral of redwoods on Bull Creek Flat, and not a single tree had a shred of protection. In the spring of 1919, several months before the group's first board meeting at the Palace, a Chicago philanthropist and devoted League supporter named Edward Ayer would liken the logging scene in that region to World War I, in particular to the horrifically devastated bombed-out fields of France.

But as the coming years were about to show, John Merriam, Henry Osborn, and Madison Grant were forces to reckon with. Their urge to do something to save the great trees was fueled by a mix of both near-religious awe and, especially in the case of Osborn and Merriam, who were both paleontologists, a lifelong commitment to science. It was not by accident that Save the Redwoods League, founded the following March with donations from industrialist Stephen Mather, Assistant Secretary of the Interior E. C. Bradley, former California congressman and philanthropist William Kent, and Osborn and Grant themselves, would forever after be populated to a significant degree by scientists—evolutionary biologists, paleontologists, geologists, and ecologists—each one answering the call to a flurry of questions sparked by these singular trees.

The redwoods impressed these science-loving League founders not only in terms of their longevity (a single tree was able to live some two thousand years) but also by the fact that tens of millions of years earlier, the trees had grown across much of what would become the United States. Clipped over countless millennia by a changing climate, ultimately they were left hugging only the very western edge of the continent, where they could quench their need for water in part by a delicate embrace of the region's morning fog. To people of science, that alone was an incredible story—a story they believed must not end with the trees being lost to the saws, sacrificed to make lumber and shingles and grape stakes.

Forty-eight-year-old John Campbell Merriam, a native of Iowa, was at the time of that trip to Bull Creek a renowned professor of paleontology at the University of California, Berkeley; much of his career had been devoted to trying to piece together the prehistoric unfolding of both the land and life of the West Coast. He was extraordinarily good at organizing. Besides heading an international relations committee at the university, he was, when the United States entered World War I in 1917, appointed by President Woodrow Wilson to head a program of war-related scientific work. In Merriam's twenty-five-year run as president of Save the Redwoods League, he would push for protection of the big trees with a compelling blend of science and poetry, on any given day weaving into conversations not just his exacting knowledge but his favorite lines from Wordsworth, Shelley, Tennyson, and Keats.

Meanwhile, geologist and paleontologist Henry Fairfield Osborn had, among a great many other things, served as curator of the American Museum of Natural History in New York, where he steered the development of what would arguably become the most famous and admired fossil display in the world. He too, though, possessed a capacity far beyond rigorous scientific thought. Of the redwoods he saw on Bull Creek, Osborn would later claim that "their venerable and colossal splendor is a heritage for the future of America."

And finally was Madison Grant, son of a respected Civil War surgeon. Though trained as a high-powered lawyer, Grant would use his love of science and his considerable inherited wealth to help found organizations from the New York Zoological Society to the American Bison Society. While Osborn and Merriam were polite, gracious, and, in the case of Merriam, somewhat reserved, Grant was flashy, and sometimes quick to quarrel. He often brought reluctant potential supporters on board by flooding them with banter, all but overwhelming them. The three men were different, to be sure, and in many areas of life they held vastly different views. But when it came to saving the greatest trees on Earth, they would act with an astonishing singularity of purpose.

Being so strongly committed to science, the League's founders—not to mention many of its early administrators—

were passionately interested in evolutionary theory. Specifically they were drawn to so-called orthogenesis, which is a kind of "straight line" theory of evolution whereby organisms are guided by internal forces that move them toward a fixed goal. Unlike the theory of random or "accidental" natural selection, progressive evolutionists see the life of the world as constantly improving toward an ordained objective. Thus, the mighty redwood was seen as the inevitable consequence of millions of years of continuous improvement. In much the same way, humans were seen as the leading edge of what was possible for mammals. That belief allowed many in the League to embrace the idea of human progress, believing our rational capacities allowed us to advance faster than we would by mere random natural selection. Progressive evolution allowed for both faith in biology as well as—at least for some—theological faith. Thus, accomplished scientist John C. Merriam also believed that by experiencing the redwoods we could "turn toward contemplation of undefined sources of being and power." It mattered not at all whether somebody wanted to save the redwoods for science, or save them for inspiration; for the followers of progressive evolution, like so many involved early on with Save the Redwoods League, it was one and the same.

Yet it's important to note that progressive evolution also had a very dark side. Through his interests as an amateur scientist, Madison Grant ended up a strong believer in a dangerous strain of thought quite popular during the early twentieth century, called eugenics. Eugenics sought to increase the "quality" of the nation's citizens both by cleansing it of "inferior races," and at the same time sterilizing those with mental or physical disabilities. (John Merriam, on the other hand, was among the many who strongly disagreed with the premises of eugenics, describing it as a profound misinterpretation of scientific principles.) Sadly, Madison Grant's writings on eugenics were destined to become fodder for some of the most nefarious men the world has ever known, including Adolf Hitler. Ironically, Grant himself would later succumb to a crippling form of arthritis—a condition that would by the standards of eugenics have rendered him a "defective" member of the human race.

Beyond their considerable skill set, the founders of the League had the good fortune to launch their efforts at a time when the stars were aligned in just the right way. For one thing, during the first two decades of the twentieth century, philanthropy was on the rise, and not just single-person, individually directed philanthropy like that of multimillionaire Andrew Carnegie. Donations were also coming in as a result of powerful, full-bodied professional fundraising—a profession that in 1918 was well on its way to becoming a fine art, thanks in part from strategies pioneered by groups such as the Red Cross and the YMCA. What's more, federal tax law had been changed, allowing corporations to deduct up to 15 percent of their taxable income as gifts to charities. That development alone was one the League would seize to wonderful effect.

Many of the early members of Save the Redwoods League and its Board of Councilors were either well-heeled, well-schooled, well-connected, or all three. Ardent League supporter Stephen Mather, for example, had in 1916 done much to enable the creation of the National Park Service by digging into his own considerable fortune to make it happen. And he had plenty of good friends in high places. When he alerted Secretary of the Interior Franklin Lane about the plight of the redwoods, Lane was so moved that he ended up becoming the League's first volunteer president, stepping into the slot during that board meeting at the Palace Hotel. Thus Save the Redwoods League grew not just through a network of people who knew what they were talking about when it came to big trees, but also through powerful politicians, financiers, media moguls, and industrialists. Among those who not only contributed themselves but also helped open the wallets and purses of similarly affluent men and women across the nation were Gilbert Grosvenor of *National Geographic,* Chicago philanthropist Edward Ayer, James Crocker of San Francisco's Crocker National Bank, and the supremely well-connected New York matriarch Helen Thorne, wife of businessman Oakleigh Thorne, to name just a few.

Some of the early League directors and councilors were progressives, others conservatives, but they all shared key ideas about how the world works. Like many philanthropists of the early industrial era, they believed in noblesse oblige—the notion that those who'd risen to the top of society should contribute both money and time to the betterment of the culture. Furthermore, most, though not all, had strong faith in the benefits of regional, decentralized government, believing that tapping into the federal largess should in most cases be a move of last resort. Later on, when it became common to purchase and preserve redwood groves by means of regional or state bond issues, which were in turn matched by private funds, many in the League believed such bonds should only be issued when private funds were already pledged.

Finally, for all their devotion to reaching out and building alliances with other groups across the economic and political spectrum—from tourism councils to scenic highway groups to garden clubs—the League wasn't inclined to have its strategies dictated by small, decentralized regional groups, as other organizations like the Sierra Club would do. Far better, they thought, to assemble the very best leadership in one place, tap into a trusted group of councilors to firm up their strategies, and then reach out to everyone they possibly could in the general public to build widespread support.

But there was something else, something quite profound, and it too would have much to do with the League's prodigious successes. This was the passionate affection for, and deep connection to, wild places that had been running through the veins of the country since its founding. For millions of people, nature—and perhaps even more so the nature to be found in forests—was seen as a priceless legacy. An unshakeable source of identity. An identity that in 1918 seemed suddenly vulnerable to being severely eroded by a fast-rising tide of industrialization.

As early as the mid-1700s, pundits in what would later become the United States were referring to wild places as "the great equalizer," so called because such landscapes were understood to hand out their blessings and inspirations, as well as their dangers, equally to all. In other words, what the nature of the continent had to offer at the highest level had nothing to do with the amount of money in your pockets or how much "blue" was in your blood; here were forests thick and vast and, more important still, not locked up behind the guarded walls of the landed gentry, as they were in much of England and Europe. Here nature was for everyone. (Tragically, though, "everyone," as it was understood at the time, left out entire groups of people, including those who'd been living on these lands for thousands of years.) Later, in 1872, Congress voted to spend the whopping sum of $10,000—this in a bad economy—to buy Thomas Moran's *Lower Falls of the Yellowstone*, which became the first landscape painting to hang in the U.S. Capitol. Those who came and saw the painting, it was argued, were bound to find their hearts reawakened to the promise of democracy.

In the late 1700s, prominent figures like patriot and future first lady Abigail Adams predicted for the country great flurries of artistic expression—an endless abundance of musicians, painters, and writers—based on the fact that we were spending so much time rubbing elbows with the woods. Appropriately, the piece of writing considered by some to be the first great work of American literature appeared in the early nineteenth century, when poet Joseph Rodman Drake penned a long verse about the forest called *The Culprit Fay*—a piece *American Monthly Magazine* called "one of the most exquisite productions in the English language." The tale was crafted around creatures known as Pukwudgies in the Wampanoag culture of present-day Massachusetts and Rhode Island—fairy-like denizens of the deep woods which Drake set against a curious mix of Arthurian legend and Celtic mysticism.

Many pundits thought that Americans didn't necessarily have to experience the unshackled forests firsthand in order to benefit from them. As the famous nineteenth-century commentator Henry George wrote, "The free, independent spirit, the energy and hopefulness that have marked our people . . . have sprung from unfenced land." The idea of parks and public nature preserves have "given a consciousness of freedom even to the dweller in crowded cities," serving as a "well-spring of hope even to those who never thought of taking refuge upon it."

As concern about the redwoods began to build in the early years of the 1900s, nature writing dominated magazines from the *Atlantic Monthly* to *Colliers*. Bookstore shelves sagged under the weight of authors like Henry David Thoreau and John Muir, John Burroughs, Ernest Thompson Seton, Teddy Roosevelt, and William Long. The enormously popular *Century Magazine* declared that the American nature movement had "no counterpart" anywhere in the world. By the time Big Basin Redwoods State Park was created in the heart of the Santa Cruz Mountains in 1902, Burroughs's books for children could be found in nearly every school in the country, and there were tens of thousands of kids waking up Christmas morning thrilled to find Seton's *Wild Animals I Have Known* waiting under the tree. In Humboldt County, the thick of redwood country, a 1908 petition to save the redwoods was signed by more two thousand schoolchildren from Eureka; soon afterward no less than President Theodore Roosevelt got wind of it, making it a point to let the children know he was eager to lend a hand.

Even the fledgling discipline of psychology was quick to throw its hat in the nature ring. As celebrated therapist G. Stanley Hall—the man who coined the term "adolescence"—made clear in 1906, "In our urban hot-house life, that tends to ripen everything before its time, we must teach nature.... Two staples, stories and nature, ... constitute the fundamental education." During its first hundred years, Save the Redwoods League would steadfastly fill that very prescription.

For all these reasons, then, it was the United States itself that to no small degree helped assure that the message of Save the Redwoods League—which was that protecting redwoods was generous, that it was critical to science, and, beyond all, that it was an act of patriotism—landed squarely in the hearts of millions of people. Again and again, through two world wars, the Great Depression, and profound social upheaval, the League would tap into such bone-deep feelings, raising hundreds of millions of dollars toward preservation of these mighty trees. Much of the effort consisted of sharing the magic of the redwoods through guided tours and lectures and with stunning photographs and passionate, poetic prose. But it was also a matter of showing how widespread was the destruction of the great forests, which Americans came to see as a heinous crime. Following one of his many visits to redwood country, Stephen Mather spoke for many in a letter to colleague Horace Albright when he said, "It is stupefying to see what destruction man is capable of. I felt almost physically sick when viewing the mortal remains of these immortal trees."

Back at the Palace Hotel, at that August 1919 meeting of the Save the Redwoods League Board of Directors, the group was fired up. Among the many things they tackled that day was coming up with a clear intent of purpose, which included the following:

a) to secure the finest and most available tract of redwood timber as a national park;

b) to secure a strip 300 yards wide or other suitable width along each side of the highway as a state park [referring to a new highway being built that connected the redwood country to more populated regions to the south];

c) to obtain by private gifts such other fine tracts of land as may be recommended by a committee appointed to make a thorough study of the redwood situation.

The first goal, to secure a national park, would take up most of the next fifty years, requiring the League to navigate unimaginably dense thickets of political intrigue. As for the other two goals—securing trees along the new "Redwood Highway" and acquiring tracts of land through private gifts—they were off and running from the very start, with lists made and wheels turning almost before the ice had melted in the bottoms of their glasses.

By autumn of the following year, Save the Redwoods League was a nonprofit California corporation, firmly planted in an organizational structure that would over the next twenty years include nearly eighty councilors from across the country—from bankers to professors to university regents to landscape architects to captains of industry. Over 85 percent of those councilors had college degrees, and over half had multiple degrees. About 20 percent of the councilors were independently wealthy.

To the great credit of the founding officers of Save the Redwoods League, it was understood—perhaps especially by John C. Merriam—that the League's success rested not just on employing good science to find the best groves of redwood to preserve, but also on clear and charismatic persuasion. Persuasion that would be applied to acquiring major donations, to be sure—but also to building a broad, eager base of public support. With that in mind, in 1919 the League hired a brilliant young public relations professional named Newton Drury, who was working in the PR profession in the San Francisco Bay Area with his brother Aubrey. In hiring Newton Drury, Save the Redwoods League embraced a big shift happening across the country, as conservation work started gaining ground not just on the say of powerful, politically connected individuals, but also through the power of public relations—a field that at the time was led by people who'd cut their teeth doing such work for the government, specifically in rallying support for World War I.

Soon after his hiring, Drury, who would later become a tireless, gracious, and much-beloved executive director of the League, set about enlisting the help of the women of Humboldt County. It was a brilliant move. The women were masterful not only at organizing but also in figuring out how to garner publicity for the redwoods. At the same time, Drury launched a brilliantly written, lavishly illustrated series of regional and national magazine and newspaper articles, and these too paid off handsomely. By the end of the organization's first year, membership had grown to more than three thousand. It grew by still another thousand in the year that followed—far outpacing any other conservation group of the day. At the end of their first decade, Save the Redwoods League's membership had swelled to seven thousand, making it the largest member-based environmental group in the United States. Famed National Park Service interpreter Freeman Tilden would later declare: "Building from a small pool of seed contributions, the League was to become one of the greatest agencies of preservation the world has ever known."

Of all the strategies employed by the fledgling Save the Redwoods League, among the most significant was the hard, patient work spent building and sustaining a broad web of relationships—with powerful politicians and wealthy funders, to be sure, but also with people who, while they may have had less notoriety, were driven by a thoroughly tenacious commitment to preserving the trees.

One of the most striking examples is the League's alliance with the California Federation of Women's Clubs—an organization that included over eight hundred women in Humboldt County alone, some of whom had been steadfastly working on saving the last of the redwoods since shortly after the turn of the century. Indeed, when Laura White founded the CFWC in 1900, it claimed two standing committees: the first was education, the second was forestry. While it's often reported that League cofounder John C. Merriam made that now legendary trip to the Bull Creek redwoods with Madison Grant and Henry Fairfield Osborn at the urging of Park Service director Stephen Mather, what's less well known is that he made the trip in part because the women of Humboldt County had alerted him through letters to the rampant logging of the big trees. Notably, these women were in many cases the wives and daughters, mothers and sisters and aunts of the loggers themselves.

Yet the members of the CFWC were much more than just fervent letter writers. They also collected data, and made their own recommendations about what trees to save. In what became the first major push to create a redwood national park, it was the Humboldt County Federation of Women's Clubs, under the guidance of Laura Perrott Mahan, that was given the task of surveying appropriate sites and estimating costs of acquiring the lands. After seeing their proposal die not once but twice in congressional committee, the women, deeply disappointed, decided to put the issue to rest until a more opportune time. Yet time and again over the coming decades, they would join forces with the League to ensure the success of key redwood preservation projects. Indeed, correspondence suggests that in its formative decades, the League was working more often with the CFWC affiliates of Northern California than with any other group.

Six days after that first Save the Redwoods League board meeting at the Palace Hotel, Madison Grant and Stephen Mather traveled to the Northern California timber town of Eureka to make their case for saving the big trees, in large part touting the benefits of tourism. The fact that they were met by an auditorium filled to the brim with enthusiastic supporters—and again, this was in the heart of logging country—was in no small extent due to the fact that the women of Humboldt County had been nurturing the idea with their neighbors for years. If the likes of John Muir and Teddy Roosevelt had sounded the clarion call from on high about the need to save the redwoods for science and tourism and national posterity, it would be Laura White, Clara Bradley Burdette, Laura Mahan, and others who, through the women's clubs of California, helped make local residents see them also as anchors for community, essential threads in the fabric of what it meant to be at home in America.

In 1923, Laura Mahan achieved the rather astonishing feat of bringing the annual meeting of the California Federation of Women's Clubs to Eureka—a major coup for this small town—in the process greatly expanding enthusiasm for the region's enchanted redwood forests. After giving attendees the chance to dine in an exquisite redwood grove known as Dyerville Flat, near the Bull Creek grove, Mahan pressed her fellow club members—many of whom were very well connected—to buy the grove in order to save it from the saws. Which is exactly what they did, creating the Federation of Women's Clubs Grove, which to this day still thrills thousands of travelers along the Redwood Highway.

Much like the League itself, the women's clubs of Humboldt County let no opportunity to call attention to the redwoods slip through their fingers. At one point they managed to get the U.S. postmaster general to agree that all outgoing mail from Humboldt County would be stamped with the message "Save the Redwoods." And it was thanks in large part to what was originally called the Women's Save the Redwoods League of Humboldt County (separate from the national preservation group in San Francisco) that a powerful documentary about the loss of the redwoods was made. Later, the Hollywood movie company known as Famous Players-Lasky (which later became Paramount) was convinced to show the documentary in theaters across the United States, tacking it onto their movie rendition of Peter Kyne's novel *The Valley of the Giants*, a dramatic tale about a timber harvester struggling to save a grove of redwoods in memory of his beloved wife.

When the first three women—Mrs. Frank G. Law, Mrs. Aaron (Adella) Schloss, and Mrs. Charles H. (Eleanor) Toll—came into the Board of Councilors of Save the Redwoods League in 1922, director J. D. Grant properly acknowledged that it was to women that "we owe very largely the success that has thus far attended our efforts."

The national Save the Redwoods League was steadfast in following a course set early on, first championed by John C. Merriam and enacted by Newton Drury. This had to do with a strong belief that the redwoods, the vast majority of which were in private hands, would be saved mostly through thoughtful, nonconfrontational effort—what Merriam called a "unity of action." And in fact many of the early donations of redwood stands in the 1920s by the companies that owned them—Hammond, Lagoon, Hobbs-Wall, the Albion Lumber Company, the Sage Land and Improvement Company, and the Southern Pacific Railroad—seemed to underscore the wisdom of that collaborative approach. And yet there were times when this path would prove challenging. Be too timid, after all, and redwoods would be unnecessarily lost. Be too aggressive, on the other hand, and not only the timber companies that owned the lands might walk away, but so too might some of the wealthy business-oriented benefactors who were so important to the effort. In short, there were enormous risks in either extreme.

Time and again the League found itself working the middle road, sustaining support from conservatives and progressives alike. It wasn't easy. In 1923, for instance, a set of three bills was introduced to the California legislature, each having to do with giving the state the authority to use eminent domain to protect treasures like redwood groves along the state's highways, as well as by creating state parks. One of the bills would've required that as soon as private funds equal to the value of a particular stand of desired redwoods were deposited in the state treasury, the state could, if the timber company refused to sell, move to condemn the land, paying out fair market value to the owner.

Many preservationists, which included some high-profile members of the League like Stephen Mather, wanted the organization to throw its growing weight behind such measures. Yet condemnation was for League directors a sketchy precedent, a last resort that had the potential to anger the very timber companies they were then negotiating with to purchase the big trees. In the end, Merriam and Save the Redwoods League declined to support the bills, while at the same time agreeing that they also wouldn't go on record opposing them.

What also bothered the League about this and other legislation, however, was that it wasn't tied to any sort of master plan that prioritized what redwood groves should be saved. Acting out of their strong and early impulse to create a thoughtful, professional master plan of park development—one that would allow condemnation only if necessary to secure the very best groves—they turned to the son of the creator of Central Park, and an enormous fan of the redwoods, Frederick Law Olmsted Jr. Olmsted went on to draw up plans to protect four different areas of the northern redwoods. Each project focused on the oldest, most beautiful stands across various ecological zones of redwood country, and, at the same time, ones easily accessible to the public.

This latter criterion especially led him to recommend groves on the flats, like Bull Creek and stretches along the nearby South Fork of the Eel River. To the north he chose an area east of Gold Bluffs Beach, along with a small oceanside grove—by then exceedingly rare—in Del Norte County. These four recommended projects represented only about 3 percent of the remaining redwood forest.

Some of the stands, like Bull Creek, would take the League almost a dozen years of painstaking effort to secure, as they were rebuffed time and again by the single owner of that grove, Pacific Lumber. But other stands of the four identified projects, including those that would become Del Norte Coast Redwoods State Park, passed through the League from a dozen different owners almost without a hitch.

The fly in the ointment was that some of the state parks fell under the jurisdiction of the State Board of Forestry, which on more than one occasion had proven itself to be in the pocket of the timber industry. Still other parks were managed by California Fish and Game, even the State Highway Commission. It was an inefficient system at best, prone to being overly provincial, often to the detriment of the good of the whole. Furthermore, acting out of its strong scientific foundation, the League felt that only an agency with trained professionals—an actual State Parks Commission—would be able to coordinate meaningful scientific and educational research. Spectacularly adept lobbying by the League led to unanimous passage of a

State Parks Commission bill in 1925.

And then Governor Friend Richardson, a staunch conservative, promptly vetoed it. But to its great credit, the League has never been inclined to take "no" as a final answer. The matter came up again in 1926 under a new and far more progressive governor, C. C. Young; and he was backed by a legislature that was even more receptive to conservation. The resulting Parks Commission was not only given the power to condemn land but was authorized to put on the ballot a $6 million bond issue to purchase lands throughout the state. A significant amount of that money would end up going to protect redwoods.

Hardly had the ink of Governor Young's signature dried before the League, working with the Sierra Club, launched what at the time was the biggest publicity campaign in California history: a bond promotion that allowed, as of 1928, public bonds for parks to be made available as soon as private matching funds had been secured. The idea drew robust energy from the California Federation of Women's Clubs, sportsmen's groups, chambers of commerce, and fraternal organizations. In the end the legislation passed in every single county, and in over half of those counties it passed with margins of two or three to one. And thus to a very large, very real extent, the League helped pave the way for the magnificent California State Parks system that millions of people delight in to this day.

By 1929, Save the Redwoods League had raised more than

$500,000 (about $7 million in today's dollars), allowing the relatively quick preservation of some three thousand acres of precious redwood forest in four stunningly beautiful parks. And by 1931, thanks in large part to a generous donation by the Rockefeller family at the eleventh hour, the fabled redwoods at Bull Creek—the grove that had so enchanted Merriam, Osborn, and Grant in 1917—were saved as well, despite having already been scheduled for cutting.

Beyond outright fundraising, the League also applied the brilliant idea of encouraging wealthy donors to secure specific stands of redwoods as memorials to friends or loved ones. The first such memorial grove, along the South Fork of the Eel River, was established in 1921 in honor of Colonel Raynal C. Bolling, the first U.S. Army officer of high rank to fall in World War I. During the first decade of the League's existence, memorial groves accounted for a whopping 30 percent of the total moneys raised. Later, at the end of World War II, League executive director Aubrey Drury put a slightly different slant on the memorial grove idea, writing an essay for the *Sierra Club Bulletin* that sparked a passionate response from people across the country:

> In every city, town, and village in this broad land of ours, people are thinking and talking and wondering what honor can be paid to those millions of men who have gone forth to do battle with the enemy for the

preservation of our beloved country, its people, and its institutions. Thus *The Eternal Gratitude of the Nation Eternally Expressed* is to be symbolized by the dedication of a grove of redwoods of great beauty and magnitude, selected upon recommendation by America's distinguished landscape architect, Frederick Law Olmsted, after a survey of the entire northern redwood belt.

The idea—presented as a progressive plan to secure ten 500-acre parcels—spread like wildfire, becoming one of the most successful preservation efforts of the decade. Thousands of donations poured in from coast to coast, from every sector of the public. No donation was considered too small. The Daughters of the American Revolution made it their mission to acquire the last of the ten parcels from the Del Norte Lumber Company, raising more than $26,000, much of it through thousands of ten-cent donations. Donors also had the option of including with their gifts the name of a veteran who fought in the war; those names were enshrined in a Golden Book—one copy kept in California, the other in Washington, D.C.

The League reaped the benefits of popular support. And then, at the dawning of the 1940s, under the calm, competent guidance of Newton Drury's brother, Aubrey, Save the Redwoods League suddenly found itself facing a major challenge. It came in the form of a proposed amendment to the California constitution known as Senate Constitutional Amendment

(SCA) 33. Arguably one of the most potentially damaging proposals in California history, SCA 33 would have allowed the state to sell off any park or preserve thought to hold oil or gas reserves. In the end, the struggle would prove once and for all that while the League was intensely collaborative, it could also unleash fiercely effective campaigns against any threat to the state's natural treasures. True to his quiet yet forceful management style, Drury not only talked with state politicians but led a remarkably powerful publicity campaign against the bill—a virtual uprising of ads and stories and lectures and political cartoons—while at the same time building channels for the general public to petition government leaders, chambers of commerce, tourism boards, and historical societies. When the smoke cleared, SCA 33 was handily defeated, voted down by the citizens of California at a rate of more than five to one.

During the middle of the twentieth century, the League also stayed true to its belief in education—going so far during the scant state budgets of the World War II years to help fund interpretive naturalists to the state parks. The group also managed to keep eyes and hearts on the giant sequoias of the state, which grow inland along the foothills of the Sierra Nevada range. In 1954, the League helped the Calaveras Grove Association acquire the south grove of giant sequoias, thereby significantly enlarging Calaveras Big Trees State Park. "Much of what we've accomplished over the last eighty years," explains Marilyn Regan, current president of the Calaveras Big Trees Association, "was due in large part to League members' generosity."

While these middle decades brought a number of leadership changes to the League, the group remained remarkably cohesive—and therefore effective—in large part by continuing to draw on those who'd been engaged since the early days. Former Eureka banker Arthur Connick, for instance, who'd been one of the League's original incorporators in 1920, went on to take the reins as president in the early '50s. Beyond his expertise about the League itself, Connick's sterling reputation among timber company owners and managers as a trustworthy, forthright businessman allowed him to be enormously effective when it came to negotiating land deals with the industry on the League's behalf.

Since the turn of the twentieth century, creating a redwood national park was a passionate concern for thousands of people, including the founding members of Save the Redwoods League. Yet the early League was savvy enough—in large part through its connections to key politicians—to understand that Congress in the 1920s, no matter how fervently petitioned, was reluctant to use tax dollars to purchase private lands for a park—a position that was very much in line with the philosophy of the League itself.

In addition to heroic work done in the early 1900s by state garden clubs and the California Federation of Women's Clubs, in 1911 Congressman John Raker tried to get a national park feasibility study done, but to no avail. (Curiously, in the following session of Congress it was Raker who crafted and sponsored the law that allowed the controversial damming of the Tuolumne River, thereby flooding the Hetch Hetchy Valley.) Later both Stephen Mather and League member William Kent (the latter of whom had with his wife, Elizabeth, in 1905 purchased Muir Woods in Marin County, preserving its old-growth redwoods as a public park) would put up $10,000 of their own money for that national park feasibility study. And still the rock wouldn't move. If a national park were to happen—or, more fundamentally, if redwood groves were going to be saved by any means—it would take continuing hard work to secure state and private money. And the fact is, no one was better at that than Save the Redwoods League.

Nearly forty years would pass before even the prospect of a national park seemed within reach. By that time, however, the social and political climate around preservation had changed profoundly. On one hand, logging of the nation's forests had increased dramatically in the 1950s, rising in part to meet demand for housing following World War II. In Humboldt and Del Norte Counties alone, the cutting of redwoods in each year of the 1950s and early '60s occurred at a rate over three times what it had been in any previous year; in Humboldt County's Redwood Creek watershed alone, the big trees fell through the decade of the '50s at the rate of three thousand trees a year. By the end of the decade just 10 percent of the original two million acres of redwoods were still standing.

Add to this a flurry of dam building, as well as pollution problems ranging from smog to the poisoning of waterways by industry to the rampant use of the insecticide DDT. Not surprisingly, given the love of nature that had inspired residents of this land for so long, there came on the scene a generation of young people convinced that preservation would happen only by aggressive, no-holds-barred media blitzes, from coffee table books to full-page ads in the *New York Times*. All of that, in turn, with sharply crafted legal challenges and full-throttle lobbying—an approach markedly different from the more restrained methods long embraced by Save the Redwoods League.

To be fair, there were times—especially during years when political leaders were friendly to the environment, which included much of the 1960s and '70s—that this new approach yielded notable victories: it kept dams out of national monuments, established healthy air- and water-quality standards, created wilderness preserves, and removed a whole host of dangerous chemicals from agriculture and manufacturing. In hindsight we could probably say that in times when political leadership was sensitive to environmental concerns, the more aggressive, confrontational strategies worked. But when the social and political climate leaned more conservative, in the direction of development, the approach taken by the League—preserving nature by patient negotiation with the stakeholders—has often been the more effective path.

In the 1960s and '70s it took stubborn courage for the League's leadership and Board of Councilors to stay the course—a stand that earned them plenty of anger and derision from more aggressive environmental groups. But this isn't to say the League didn't evolve. This was especially true when it came to embracing new perspectives being opened by scientific research. For example, their original preference for protecting the biggest, best redwoods, and the ones easily accessible by road, would with the rise of ecology yield to a willingness to embrace the more complicated task of securing watersheds, as well as larger, more diverse biotic systems. That kind of evolution within the organization actually fit seamlessly into the League's top two priorities for redwood-based state parks, as articulated years earlier by John C. Merriam. First, he advised the group, be concerned about the spiritual and aesthetic experiences of visitors. Next, preserve the scientific and educational values of those same preserves.

Even before the science of ecology had taken hold in the public consciousness—encouraged by the writings of scientists such as Aldo Leopold and Rachel Carson—nature herself taught the League some important lessons about interdependence. In the 1920s, for example, the Rockefeller family had given an incredible $2 million to help secure the magnificent redwoods growing on the flats around Bull Creek, that magic grove that had so inspired the founders of the League and that later became part of Humboldt Redwoods State Park. What didn't get preserved at the time, and thus what ended up exposed to unregulated, unrestrained logging, were the forests standing on the steep slopes in the upper reaches of the watershed. During a season of unusually heavy rains in the winter of 1954–55, parts of those ravaged, denuded upper slopes let loose, washing thousands of tons of soil, as well as large piles of cut logs and other debris, into the creek. The force of the flow was astonishing. By the end of those debris slides, some fifty acres of the precious Bull Creek Flat had been carried away. And more appalling still, more than five hundred redwood trees were lost. The lesson was clear. In the decades that followed, the League devoted itself to helping the state acquire steep slopes in several locations above the flats that held the critical signature groves.

History suggests that when it comes to the two approaches to preservation mentioned earlier—one patient and collaborative, the other more aggressive, founded on legal challenge and edgy, insistent marketing—each has its place. But fostering collaborations between groups that embrace those different strategies can sometimes be like trying to mix oil and water. When it came to the creation of a Redwoods National Park, to no small degree it was disagreement among preservation groups themselves—characterized most clearly by the clash between Save the Redwoods League and the Sierra Club, each standing on profoundly different philosophical ground—that helped make the road to a national park even longer and more tortured than it might have otherwise been.

In 1963, Secretary of the Interior Stewart Udall made a public pledge of support for the national park idea. Unfortunately, he did so without having completed the necessary survey to determine exactly which lands such a park should include. Save the Redwoods League pushed hard for a site at Mill Creek, near Crescent City, while the Sierra Club felt Redwood Creek, located about forty miles to the south, near Orick, to be the better choice. In large part because of connections established long before by Save the Redwoods League, the National Geographic Society stepped in with $64,000 to complete the survey work.

Stumping to Congress for the plan to locate the park on Mill Creek, as the League preferred, was Laurance Rockefeller, who not only had the ear of President Johnson but was a longtime supporter of Save the Redwoods League (as was his father, John D. Rockefeller Jr., who had, among other conservation efforts, helped save the Bull Creek redwoods in the early '30s). Indeed, early League director Newton Drury had by this time served as a trusted conservation advisor to the Rockefellers for more than thirty years. Rockefeller not only liked the Mill Creek option for its astonishing beauty but agreed with the League that it would provoke less of a fight with the timber industry and their employees in Del Norte County than would a larger park on Redwood Creek. The Mill Creek plan, as Udall described it, capturing a consistent stance of the League, was "the art of the possible."

In the spring of 1966, bills were introduced in the House and Senate for a 39,000-acre national park that would include both Jedediah Smith and Del Norte Coast Redwoods State Parks, along with a 1,600-acre stand of big trees on Redwood Creek. Angered by the plan, the Miller Redwood Company immediately began intensive logging along the eastern boundary of Jedediah Smith State Park, cutting a five-hundred-foot-wide strip in the upper Mill Creek watershed along the park boundary. Udall called it "spite cutting," and even many in the timber industry thought that a fair description. In response, California senior senator Thomas Kuchel introduced a resolution to prohibit for a year Miller Redwood's ability to cut in those places being considered for national park protection. Simpson Lumber, meanwhile, frustrated by the bad publicity coming to the entire industry from Miller's act of defiance, contacted Senator Henry Jackson and, along with the Arcata and Georgia-Pacific companies, agreed to a one-year moratorium on cutting.

The League, meanwhile, kept urging for a united front among conservationists in supporting the Mill Creek plan for a national park. But the Sierra Club, growing in power and influence, and still thoroughly convinced that the Redwood Creek site was the better location, declined. In the end, Congress adjourned with national park plans dying in committee.

In early winter, the League issued a press release: Having assessed the damage done by Miller Redwood, they confessed that while their goal had been to preserve in a primal state the Mill Creek watershed, "We have waited too long." The following month, the League issued another statement, this time saying that either Mill Creek or Redwood Creek would be acceptable for a national park. The next proposal coming from the Johnson administration pushed for the Mill Creek site, but at the same time called for a second preserve of 17,000 acres on Redwood Creek, to be acquired entirely by private donations.

Frustrated by the schism among the preservationists themselves, in 1967 the Senate Committee on Interior and Insular Affairs proposed a two-unit park of more than 61,000 acres, embracing the best stands along both Redwood Creek and Mill Creek. The primary redwood preservation groups—Save the Redwoods League and the Sierra Club—gave it their support. Governor Ronald Reagan declared he would back a slightly smaller two-unit park of 57,000 acres. Finally, it looked like success was within reach.

And yet more stumbling blocks lay ahead. In June of 1968, Wayne Aspinall's House Interior Committee shocked everyone by introducing a redwood national park bill protecting just 28,500 acres, to be made up almost entirely of lands already held in state parks. With Congress about to adjourn, and against very real fears by preservationists that the next congressional session might prove harsher still, the bill passed, though with an assurance from Aspinall that the park area would be increased in conference committee. Which it was. By the time the park bill cleared committee, it contained two units totaling 58,000 acres, of which just under 11,000 acres were old-growth redwoods. At a final price tag of $198 million, it was the most expensive purchase of national park lands in the nation's history.

The national park wasn't perfect, by any means, and the League immediately set about trying to make it better. Amidst blatant clear-cutting near the national park, in areas visible from the Redwood Highway, the League, in a move that broke somewhat from its tradition of steering clear of condemnation by the federal government, pledged $1 million to help the Department of the Interior acquire a buffer of redwoods near the roadway along a tributary of Redwood Creek called Skunk Cabbage Creek. (Years earlier the League had offered Arcata Redwood Lumber full market value of $15 to $20 million for the bulk of redwoods along Skunk Cabbage Creek. The gesture hadn't even garnered a reply.)

Later, struggling to better protect the groves near the southern unit of the new national park, in 1976 the League raised $1 million to buy lands near the celebrated Tall Trees Grove; once again, though, the company refused to sell. Increasingly stymied, and with John B. Dewitt succeeding Newton Drury as executive director of Save the Redwoods League, the group took yet another tentative step toward aligning efforts with the federal government, this time throwing their support behind a plan launched by the Carter administration to expand the national park. After countless rounds of negotiations, including offering $40 million in compensation to timber industry employees for lost wages due to the park expansion, Redwood National Park was increased by 48,000 acres, with an additional 30,000 acres for upstream protection standing by should they be required. Nearly 9,000 acres of old-growth redwoods were saved, bringing the total of protected lands around Redwood Creek to about 70,000 acres, in what set still another record for the most expensive land acquisition in history.

The remaining decades of the twentieth century brought loud, bright explosions of protest and corporate swashbuckling to the redwoods, much of it involving old growth owned by Pacific Lumber (the original owner of the Bull Creek grove)—in particular, a tract of old-growth redwoods known as the Headwaters Forest, in southern Humboldt County. Beginning in 1987, the group calling itself "North Coast California Earth First!," under the leadership of Darryl Cherney, Greg King, and Judi Bari, launched a series of protests to preserve the virgin redwoods, including some rather famous redwood tree-sitting events—moves that the media gobbled up with enthusiasm, but that earned them no end of enmity from the timber industry.

Cherney and the Earth Firsters were buoyed to no small degree by the hostile takeover in 1986 of Pacific Lumber, at the hands of one of the most notorious junk-bond corporate raiders in American history: Wall Street bright boy Charles Hurwitz of the Maxxam corporation. As he was wont to do, Hurwitz swallowed up Pacific Lumber in stunning fashion, acquiring control of the company through a flood of junk bonds to support still another planned takeover, this time of Kaiser Aluminum. To pay off the junk bonds, he initiated a frenzied selling off of Pacific Lumber assets, including much of the employee pension funds. He also sold off the redwoods themselves (at the time, a virgin redwood was selling for about $150,000)—more than doubling the annual cut.

Soon, high-profile celebrities began jumping into the fray. In September, singers Bonnie Raitt and Don Henley of the Eagles were arrested during a large protest in front of Pacific Lumber's Carlotta mill. They'd come as part of some four thousand people opposing pending logging in what had become the last large, privately owned virgin stand of redwoods in the United States: the Headwaters Forest—60,000 acres of virgin and second-growth timber, all owned by Maxxam. Two months later, in November 1996, actor Woody Harrelson and eight others brought rush-hour traffic to a halt on the Golden Gate Bridge in San Francisco, using climbing gear to scale suspension cables and hang banners protesting the cutting of the redwoods. The largest one read: "Hurwitz:

Aren't ancient redwoods more precious than gold?"

In 1997, a protest against cutting the last big trees in the Headwaters Forest drew nine thousand people, becoming the largest environmental protest in U.S. history. In the end, in 1999, under direction from the Clinton administration, some 10,000 acres of the Headwaters Forest were purchased for $480 million, to be set aside as a nature preserve. The deal also included a fifty-year plan for forest management—a so-called Habitat Conservation Plan—on other forestlands held by Pacific Lumber.

Even with this infusion of money, though, by 2005 the company, unable to make payments on more than $700 million in debt, and also being pursued for fraud by Humboldt County, filed for bankruptcy protection. Hurwitz blamed restrictions on redwood harvests in the Headwaters Forest. Sinking far and sinking fast, a bid to acquire Pacific Lumber was made by the Mendocino Redwood Company; another, ultimately unsuccessful bid was made by a consortium of conservation groups spearheaded by Save the Redwoods League.

True to their history, which by this point spanned almost ninety years, through this dense thicket of corporate and political intrigue, Save the Redwoods League kept up the more quiet work of saving other critical stands. In 2002, under executive director Katherine Anderton, the League at long last secured the sprawling 25,000-acre Mill Creek Forest adjacent to Redwood National Park—the largest acquisition in the group's history. While most of the land purchased had by then been thoroughly logged, the move achieved the critical goal of securing the watershed, allowing restoration efforts that would protect not just the nearby big trees but the endangered fish and wildlife, too. At around the same time, the League helped secure more than 7,000 glorious acres at Mendocino Headlands State Park. Notably, it also became a key force in developing sustainable timber harvest certification. This program, still in place today, sets guidelines for ensuring that the growth of new and existing trees is always greater than the biomass of the trees harvested.

While today, under the direction of president Sam Hodder, Save the Redwoods League remains thoroughly committed to collaborative conservation, its work has blossomed to also include critical restoration and protection projects, such as the Prairie Creek watershed in Redwood National and State Parks. While astonishing groves of old-growth redwood abound in this area, the main corridor of Prairie Creek itself, which has long been in private hands, is a former site of heavy logging and milling activity that threatened fragile species like coho salmon. Working with the National Park Service and other nonprofit conservation groups, the League is restoring the old mill site, acquiring critical linkage properties in the area, and at the same time re-creating important wetlands along the creek.

Other restoration projects include the astonishing candelabra-shaped redwoods of Shady Dell, on California's "Lost Coast"—an area reopened in 2016 after having been unavailable to the public for a hundred years.

The League is also hard at work building educational and even scientific programs in a way that keeps the public engaged with the redwoods. Some of these efforts involve celebrating the trees in the media, using films and lectures and magazine articles to introduce Americans to the value of old-growth redwoods. Other projects are quieter, though precious in their own way, such as when the League teamed up with California State Parks in 2017 to offer free day passes to the parks for those seeking alternatives to the post-Thanksgiving shopping frenzy of Black Friday.

And finally, the League remains strongly committed to supporting rigorous science. The Redwoods and Climate Change Initiative (RCCI), for example, is helping scientists establish and monitor plots throughout redwood country; from these plots researchers will document local weather and measure factors affecting tree survival—recording changes going on in wood production, carbon storage, and biodiversity. Related to these investigations, in 2013 the group sponsored the Redwood Ecology and Climate Symposium, an event that drew attention from around the world.

As of this writing, the League is also involved in a fascinating partnership with the University of California and Johns

Hopkins University to sequence the coast redwood and giant sequoia genomes. (The genome of a coast redwood, by the way, is some ten times larger than that of a human being.) By the end of this project, scientists will have determined the level of genetic diversity in the redwoods—knowledge that will in turn allow managers to restore resilience to the redwoods in the face of growing environmental challenges.

Here at the hundred-year mark, the tireless work of Save the Redwoods League has protected 220,000 acres of redwoods, and at the same time played a major role in creating sixty-six redwood parks; in fact, more than 60 percent of the redwoods in California's state parks are groves protected by the direct actions of the League. Meanwhile, an astonishing 477,000 kids have been served by League-sponsored education programs. Since 2000, the League has awarded over three hundred grants to park associations, schools, and nonprofits to further educate people about these incredible forests.

These days it can be hard to imagine that the coast redwoods of California would've ever needed such a dogged, politically and socially brilliant effort to save them in the first place. At a time when our pleasures are increasingly engineered through a circus of virtual technology, to come to the feet of the redwoods—each big tree a million tons of grace and nobility whose reign on this Earth of some 144 million years seems to shatter time itself—we might imagine that the inherent worth of such life would have naturally been given the reverence and respect it deserves.

But the coast redwoods that in 1840 sprawled like a coven of giants from south of Big Sur all the way to the hushed hills of southern Oregon fell in remarkably short order. Even with the fierce dedication of groups like Save the Redwoods League, today barely 5 percent of those two million acres of redwood stands remain. But much as wildfire tends to burn in patterns that leave small islands of seed trees, these remaining redwoods are not just seeding future redwood forests but, just as important, seeding in the human heart the wonder and awe and humility that keep us searching for how to live more sustainably on this precious planet. Of all Earth's wonders, the redwoods have proven to be especially potent wellsprings of such inspiration—able even now to wipe clean the detritus of media and politics and traffic and the little screens of our smartphones, giving us the eyes and heart with which to perceive the miraculous.

For all the strong, steadfast role nature has played in defining American character, too often we've carried no mutually agreed-on tenet to leave as sanctuary that which is truly extraordinary. We have depended on, and greatly benefited from, the enormous inspiration and commitment of men and women like those of Save the Redwoods League. These are the people who react to the astonishing in nature

Portola Redwoods State Park. Photo: Paolo Vescia.

Candelabra tree, Shady Dell, Sinkyone Wilderness State Park. Photo: Mike Shoys.

Save the Redwoods League's Ladies Committee touring Humboldt County, 1919. Photo: Freeman Art Company. Courtesy of the Humboldt County Historical Society.

Big Basin Redwoods State Park. Photo: Max Forster.

Montgomery Woods State Park. Photo: Max Forster.

Humboldt Redwoods State Park. Photo: Mike Shoys.

Harold Richardson Redwoods Reserve. Photo: Mike Shoys.

Sequoia National Park. Photo: Max Forster.

Harold Richardson Redwoods Reserve. Photo: Mike Shoys.

Del Norte Coast Redwoods State Park. Photo: Jon Parmentier.

Harold Richardson Redwoods Reserve. Photo: Mike Shoys.

Jedediah Smith Redwoods State Park. Photo: Max Forster.

Prairie Creek Redwoods State Park. Photo: Max Forster.

not just by celebrating it, but by devoting their lives to making sure it will persist for generations to come—for the sake of humans, to be sure, but also in service of the idea that a life form so astonishingly singular should be given the very best chance of survival. Because of their efforts, we can push forward into this new century able still to walk and wonder among these, the greatest trees on Earth.

Award-winning author **GARY FERGUSON** *has written for a variety of national publications and is the author of twenty-seven books on nature and science. His recent works include* The Eight Master Lessons of Nature *and* Full Ecology: Repairing Our Relationship with the Natural World, *written with his wife, social scientist Dr. Mary M. Clare.*

The Ancient Ones
Greg Sarris

There was a woman who wanted to teach me love medicine. Well, there was a man before her, but she was the first to give me a song and ingredients, the most potent of which, in addition to quail droppings, was the golden red pitch from a redwood tree. The older the tree, the better; the pitch from an old tree is richer, more powerful, principally because, as this woman had told me, it contains a longer memory of the forest.

Descriptions of indigenous peoples' use of the redwood tree abound. Coast redwoods, the tallest and among the oldest trees on earth, are unique to a relatively narrow stretch of land bordering the coast from what we call today southern Oregon down to the Monterey peninsula. Dozens of indigenous nations inhabited—and still inhabit—the region. Surely these people and their distinct cultures coevolved with the magnificent trees. The Yurok and Wiyot of northwestern California split square planks from the trees' durable wood for their houses, and from the same hard wood they crafted seafaring canoes. The deep, swift-moving Klamath River was an important travel route for many of the northwestern California Indian nations, and only canoes dug out from the trunks of heavy redwood ensured safety crossing the river and traveling its great length. My people, the Southern Pomo and Coast Miwok of Sonoma and Marin Counties, removed slabs of bark from the trees and leaned the slabs against a center pole to build conical houses, called *kotchas* by the Coast Miwok. Southern Pomo called the slabs of bark *cashi-da*, house skin. Smaller slabs were used to construct acorn granaries, the hard, impenetrable redwood protecting the acorns from pests and rodents and keeping them free from mildew. The hollow of a redwood trunk could also be used to store acorns, as long as the damp ground was covered by rocks and a layer of bay laurel leaves. Young children were known to make dolls from the hairy bark. In his *Ethnographic Notes on the Southwestern Pomo* (1967), ethnographer James Gifford noted even more uses: "The new foliage, warmed in the fire, was applied as a poultice for earache. The gummy sap which accumulated at the bottom of a hollow redwood was also taken as medicine for a run-down condition. It was soaked in water and the liquid was drunk as a tonic."

Nowhere in any of the literature I've read, however, is there mention of the sap used for love medicine. "You mustn't tell anyone we are talking about this," the woman said to me, I felt as much to warn me as to see if I could be trusted.

I was an adult, in my forties, and I knew better. I shouldn't have let myself get into this position with her in the first place. Worse, when she had broached the subject, I'd encouraged her: I listened. "Listen," she began. "When I was a young woman, my husband left me for another woman—a girl up north who was much prettier than me. And he was unkind about it. He told me, 'You, girl, aren't pretty. I will get tired of you. Her, I'll never be able to get enough of.' Shortly thereafter, my old aunt, who knew what had happened, approached me. 'You want him back?' she asked. She already knew my answer—and I already knew what she could teach me. It was raining hard, I remember. She looked out the window at the rain—we were living on the old reservation—and she said, 'In four days there will be sun. Then we will go to the redwoods. We will go to the redwoods first where it is dark at noon.'"

I got caught by her story. I'd heard rumors about this woman, about the dangerous powers she possessed. "Don't take anything to eat or drink from her," a relative warned. "Don't let her get a strand of your hair." The old-timers—and still a few Indians today—use the term *poison* for medicine that can cause ill effects in another, whether that means making one act against one's will or causing sickness or even death. Sometimes a person like that would use charmstones—oblong objects carved from quartz or various other hard rocks. To cast a spell, a poisoner might touch you with the charmstone or simply point it in your direction. A poisoner might also have a song, or a series of songs referred to as "mates." Often, casting a spell required a combination of things: powerful objects, songs, and herbs and other substances taken from the plant world. The first person who offered to teach me love medicine was an old man who lived in town, around the corner from Indian friends I'd been visiting. He'd extended his hand to me, and resting on his open palm was a beautifully polished green oblong stone.

Ethnographers, archeologists, and the like have their theories of how our people came to this continent. One popular story is that we migrated over the Bering Strait ten thousand years ago, during the last ice age. Theories also get revised. Skeletal remains found in Central America suggest we were here twenty thousand years before the Bering Strait was crossable, and recent discoveries of crudely manufactured tools in Florida and San Diego suggest our ancestors lived here in small tribes at the same time the Neanderthal inhabited caves in southern France. But who's counting?

While studying the language of the Kashaya Pomo in the late 1950s, U.C. Berkeley linguist Robert Oswalt collected a story from a tribal elder telling of a time when the ocean rose and a whale lived at the mouth of the Gualala River. The coastal people retreated from the rising water and, traveling inland to high mountains, settled in caves until the water receded. Oswalt translated the story into English and classified it in his study, *Kashaya Texts* (1964), as a myth. A few years later, geologists studying the river basin discovered the fossil remains of a whale that dated back ten thousand years, to when the same river basin was an inland ocean bay. Carbon-dated materials, such as charcoal found in the caves of Northern California's Mount Saint Helena, indicate people lived in the caves at or near the same time. Did we once look west from the mountaintop and watch the redwoods return above the water?

But of course the redwoods were here long before we were. Fossil records indicate that relatives of today's redwoods existed 160 million years ago, during the Jurassic era; some scientists interpret the data differently and suggest the trees' ancestors were here 240 million years ago. Most agree that redwoods have been in their present range, from southern Oregon to the Monterey peninsula, for at least 20 million years. And this is the only place on earth the redwood trees are found—trees that can live for two thousand years and reach heights of over three hundred feet. They no doubt loomed large in the ancient cultures of aboriginal Californians.

In the northwestern and central regions of the state, we belonged to small nations of between one thousand and five thousand individuals, each nation often comprising subgroups of related families. At the time of European contact, in the mid-1700s, there were more people in central California than anywhere else in the New World outside of the Aztec capital, Tenochtitlán, the site of present-day Mexico City, and numerous languages were spoken across the region. Most language families found in the New World as a whole were at some point found in California, and it wasn't unusual for a person to be conversant in several dialects, each one from a distinct language group. Coast Miwok is a member of the Penutian language family, for instance, whereas Pomo is a Hokan language, as dissimilar from Coast Miwok as English is from Urdu. Villagers across the creek might speak a completely different language from their nearest neighbors.

Because national territories were small—and boundaries strictly observed—tribes took great care not only of their relationships with other groups of people but also of their relationship with the land. No part of the landscape was unknown to aboriginal Californians, and they managed their resources carefully. We knew where quail nested, and we kept waterways clear of brush for ducks and geese, both to encourage the migratory waterfowl to nest and to make hunting them easier. Sedge roots were thinned and pruned to grow longer, stronger fibers for basket making, and the land was regularly burned for a variety of reasons related to the plants and animals we depended on for survival. One of the first laws the Spanish explorers and settlers imposed on us was against controlled burning, as they believed we were setting the land on fire to starve their livestock. In fact, we practiced controlled burning for a number of reasons, one of the most important being for the health of the oak trees, which gave us the acorn, our staple food. Fire destroyed larvae on the ground that would otherwise become moths that would infest the acorns and decimate the harvest. We also used controlled burning to enrich grasslands for herds of elk, pronghorn, and deer that thrived on open plains and hillsides, and we burned to control underbrush, not only so that grasslands and large trees might thrive but also to prevent wildfires we could not control.

And here I have to pause. Only two weeks ago I was evacuated from my home on Sonoma Mountain at the beginning of the historic North Bay firestorm that claimed more than 150,000 acres across Sonoma, Napa, and Solano Counties in October 2017. Over nine thousand structures were lost, including three thousand homes in Santa Rosa alone. Forty-two people died and, at the time of this writing, a dozen are still missing. The fire burned young redwood trees, but the region's ancient trees, located out of the fire's range, were unaffected. My father's cousin, a woman near ninety, offered, "Them trees won't go, don't worry. They ain't going anyplace. They been here long as us—and they'll be here long as us." Scars on old-growth trees and stumps show the trees have withstood fires before. The thick bark and hard, decay-resistant wood—one of the features that made the trees so attractive to early American loggers—protects them not only from fire and flood but also from disease. No known insect can destroy a redwood tree. Even when a tree is severely damaged, or even cut down, clones often sprout from the base, and the same tree is then able to live again and again.

The natives in the coastal regions of central California—I'm thinking principally of my people, the Southern Pomo and Coast Miwok—seldom ventured far into the redwood forests. For a host of reasons, we regarded the tall trees with great respect, even fear. The forests were so dense, the trees so tall, that before long you could find yourself in total darkness. Amidst countless and similar-looking trunks, you might quickly become lost, unable to see a way out. The dark forests were home to grizzly bears, the most powerful creatures of the land and, at that time, more numerous than people. Other animals knew as much and stayed away. Settlers discovered that they could rush elk and pronghorn to the line of a redwood forest for easy slaughter because the animals would not go into the trees. The Southern Pomo word for a redwood tree is *qasil*. For the forest, often a simple noun is used: *du-weli*, meaning night.

The landscape was our sacred text, and we listened to what it told us. Everywhere you looked there were stories. An outcropping of rocks was what had become of a greedy man's cache of elk meat. Two disrespected women turned themselves into canyon walls impossible to climb. Everything, even a mere pebble, was thought to have power—power an individual could not utilize unless he or she had a special relationship with the pebble. Violation of any aspect of the natural world—people included—would be punished, in some cases even by death. Physical violence was considered the lowest form of warfare; if you struck a person, you only demonstrated to others you had no spiritual power. Cutting down a tree was also considered a violent act. Early ethnographers characterized our culture as being predicated on black magic and fear; but might we not see it for what it was: predicated on profound respect and a fundamental belief that no one of us is the center of the universe? Doesn't this humility help explain how so many people living so close together and speaking so many different languages maintained for so long their sustainable relationships with both one another and the land?

When white people came to the area, we saw how much their values differed from ours. The Kashaya Pomo word for white people is *pala-cha*, or miracles, and an elder told me the reason: When white people entered this land, they killed humans, they killed animals, and they chopped down trees, but instead of getting punished, instead of this violence turning back on them, more white people arrived and the violence continued. We thought they were miraculous. Those ancestors who first encountered Europeans, if only they could see the world today. Not so miraculous after all. The same elder had prophesied that one day white people would come to us to "learn our ways in order to save the earth and all living things.

They will want to know [because] they will want to help. I think that day is here. You young people must not forget the things us old ones is telling you."

When we went into the redwoods, we did so with purpose. We gathered huckleberries and ferns from clearings inside the forest; mushrooms and clover too. We snared rabbits in nets beneath huckleberry bramble. Known routes through the trees connected inland valleys and plains to the ocean, and we used them with caution. Certain people had greater knowledge of the redwoods than others and therefore took more liberties. Human Bears, for instance—individuals who, having been carefully selected and secretly trained by elder cult members, donned grizzly bear hides and were endowed with the strength of the bear—traveled great distances at night through the trees, but even they were careful. There was much to be wary of. There was a tribe of Little People in the forest, humans only two feet tall, rarely amicable, easily irritated. Slug Woman lived in the forest too. At night, near the edge of the woods, you might hear the tinkling of abalone pendants attached to the empty baby cradle she carries or, worse, you might catch sight of the glistening shells. Don't follow, lest she lead you into the trees, only to return you with no memory.

The Little People and Slug Woman have been in the redwood forests a long time. Coyote planted them there when he created the world from the top of Sonoma Mountain with the assistance of his nephew Chicken Hawk. At that time, all of the animals and birds and plants and trees were people. Redwood trees were old people in Coyote's village. They were wise because they were the oldest. It is said that when they took the form of trees, they made themselves the color of blood because they wanted to remind us that we are all the same, that we were all people once from the same village on Sonoma Mountain. They went west and grew tall so we could see them and their red color and remember the story.

Growing up, I never thought much about redwood trees. They were there, like oak trees, like Santa Rosa Creek, like cars, like Jersey and Holstein cows in the fields outside of town. I worked on dairies as a small kid, and once, searching for a lost heifer—I must've been six or seven—I wandered into a grove of redwoods. Looking back, I know that the trees must've been relatively young, but I remember now how quickly the forest became dark, and then how I found the heifer, with buzzards perched on her bloated body and stiff legs, halted in their feeding to look at me.

I didn't think of redwood trees when the old man offered me his charmstone. If he was going to mention redwood pitch, I never gave him the chance. He called me from the street as I was making my way to my friend's house around the corner, and though I was only fifteen years old, I should've known better than to approach him. The unshaven, crotchety old codger sold heroin, and we'd seen twenty-year-old girls, presumably addicts, traipse in and out of his house. Sitting in the shade of his front porch, he said to me something along the lines of what he might've said to any potential initiate: "You'll be able to get anyone you want with this stone." I felt, looking at the oblong object in his hand, as if he were asking me to fondle him.

I didn't know then that I was Indian, but I'd heard Indian stories, and even witnessed some of the unbelievable things described in them. My friends—the same ones who lived around the corner from the old man—had a great-uncle who, they said, could turn into a hummingbird and travel at great speed. He was a large man, heavy set, and he wore a Stetson hat and, even on warm days, a thick overcoat. One day as a gaggle of us teenagers piled into a car, he waved at us from the front door. Five minutes later, we were stopped at a red light uptown and there he was, waving from a park bench. Strange—like so many of the Indian stories I'd heard. When the old man offered me the charmstone, I didn't think of him as being someone like my friends' great-uncle, someone who might have had ancient knowledge or powers. He didn't seem like anyone in the stories I'd heard. I tried to forget about him.

Mabel McKay was the first person I told about the encounter. She was telling me stories for her book when the memory surfaced. (I'd known her son Marshall since junior high school, but little did I know his mother was a renowned Pomo medicine woman and basket weaver, or that twenty years later I would write a book about her life, *Weaving the Dream* [1994]). It was late, near midnight, and she'd been talking for hours. She didn't like the tape recorder; she wanted me to listen. She mentioned something about a Mexican Indian shaman she'd met recently, and when she fished a glassy quartz crystal from under a clutter of coiled sedge roots and redbud bark that she used for basket making and then pushed the crystal across her kitchen table to me, I not only regained my focus but instantly thought of the charmstone in the old man's open palm. I told her what I could remember from twenty years before, describing the stone and what the man had said. Given his age at the time of our encounter, I was certain he had died by then. Mabel, however, talked to me—warned me—as if his offer still stood.

"Here's the deal," she began. "Them poisons is old—that kind of poison to get people you want, it's old. That's why they use ancient things to put in it. But here's the deal: Once you agree to use the poison, you have to agree not to forget. Sometimes you can sell it to people. But, no matter what, a person can't die until he passes it on to someone else. That's the rule."

"So he was offering me love medicine," I said. "Maybe he wanted to die."

"I don't know," Mabel said after a minute.

She told me she knew the man. She told me that she'd heard

he'd killed his first wife, that he'd drowned her in Tomales Bay. I recognized the woman's name—she was my grandmother's cousin. "You see," Mabel said, "here's the other thing: Yes, you can get anyone you want, but then you are stuck with them for everlasting. That's the power of the ingredients. Yeah, they use sap from the redwood trees. It makes the memory stick . . . I don't do them things, but that's what I heard."

Mabel sat back in her chair. She adjusted her modish glasses and looked at me. Then she started chuckling. "You don't need it," she said. "Try the regular way. You're good-looking enough."

She leaned forward and picked up the crystal, displaying it in her open hand. "Why did that Mexican Indian doctor give that to you?" I asked. "What's it for?"

She laughed out loud, uproariously. Then she stopped. With the crystal still in her hand, and just before she burst out laughing again, she said, "It's to keep you awake. You was falling asleep."

So I knew. When the woman with the love medicine made her offer and told me its ingredients and chanted its song, I knew what she wasn't telling me, the commitment I'd have no choice but to keep if I were to accept her offer. I'd heard the stories about her, yes; but I figured that with what I knew—and what I wasn't telling her I knew—I could keep one step ahead of her. She'd asked me to her cottage outside of Sebastopol, saying she was concerned about how elders had been treated at the Indian Health Clinic. While she was not enrolled in my tribe, she was a relative, and I felt compelled to hear her out. She'd finished talking about her unfaithful husband and her old aunt's offer, which I assumed she'd accepted, and I was expecting to hear about the two of them going to the redwoods where it is dark at noon, but instead she began chanting, and in English of all things.

Your name is on my lips
Your name is on my lips
Your name is on my lips
Your name is on my lips

Your name is on my lips
Your name is on my lips
Your name is on my lips
Your name is on my lips

"That's the song my old aunt taught me. She said, 'You have to hear it first.'"

Okay, I thought. She's trying to trap me, singing the song thinking she's caught me off guard. But why in English? Did the song work the same in English? And why me? Mabel told me anyone with powers to pass on—and especially poisoners—often look for a certain kind of person. They want the lonely and scared people who need to attach themselves to something in this world. At the time I had encountered the old man and his stone, I was more or less lost. I didn't know who my father was. I didn't know I was Coast Miwok and Pomo. But now I was chairman of my tribe, the Federated Indians of Graton Rancheria. I had power and influence. Wasn't that why this woman had invited me to her house in the first place?

"So what happened at the clinic?" I asked quickly, changing the subject.

I'd interrupted her and, easily enough, she lost her train of thought and launched into how difficult it was to make an appointment at the clinic, how rude the operators had been to the elders.

I felt rude myself then. I should've at least asked her about the song, about how it sounded in Pomo. I understood some Pomo. I could have let her talk. But then no, what was I thinking? I'd only encourage her. Perhaps she was sick. Perhaps she was going to die. Was that why she was trying to pass on her love medicine to me? She was not too old—fiftyish, spry, it seemed. Her shock of graying hair was cut stylishly at her ears. Her color was good, her eyes shone. She moved in her chair with ease. Did she want to tell me she needed extra attention at the clinic on account of some undisclosed disease she'd been diagnosed with?

"And listen to this," she quipped. "A woman—a friend of mine—made an appointment and when she got to the clinic, they didn't even have it written down, and they were rude to her, making her feel like she was crazy, like she had Alzheimer's disease. It's not for me, you know. I'm fine. I'm concerned about the old people. They wanted me to talk to you," she finished, dispelling my theories about her health.

But if she *had* wanted to talk to me about the clinic, how in the world had we gotten on the topic of love medicine? Had it been related to her telling me about an elder shortly after I'd sat down with her? I couldn't remember. I hadn't been paying close enough attention. Feeling generous, I turned the conversation back around. I figured I'd get her to the end of her story and then be done with it.

"So did it work, the love medicine? Did you get your husband back?"

"Oh," she laughed, as if she too had just remembered what we'd been talking about. "Listen, that fool started showing up everywhere. He'd come to my back door at night and cry, 'Please take me back. Please, my sweetheart.' Ha! One time I was at the movies downtown and I turned around and found him in the seat behind me. What did I do right in the middle of the movie? I bent over and said out loud, 'Kiss my ass.'"

I laughed. Then she picked up the story where she'd left off.

"So I went there, to the redwoods, with my aunt. They was big trees, all right." She paused, then looked away from me to the window before saying what I took as a blatant offer.

"They're there yet, them big trees. There's big trees yet by the Russian River."

When she said no more, I started talking again about potential changes to the health clinic's governing board and how that might help the situation there, and before I left, she thanked me for taking the time to hear her concerns. "The old people will be happy," she said. At the door, smiling, she thanked me again.

Later that afternoon, after reporting the woman's concerns to the health clinic, I drove to Wohler Bridge on the Russian River. Across the bridge, on the north side of the water, is a stand of redwoods, certainly not first- or second-growth trees, but tall enough. These were the trees that had come to mind when the woman mentioned redwoods and the Russian River. In the '70s, before the river was dammed a few miles downstream, clothing-optional sunbathers enjoyed a stretch of sandy beach not far from the bridge, and osprey, magnificent in the blue sky, followed the length of the river. The water was clear and shallow enough for a person to wade to the trees on the other side. The trees looked dark, a wall of trunks and thick foliage on the riverbanks. The temperature inside the stand felt cool, even cold at times, no matter how warm the summer day. Once, a friend, barefoot and naked in the trees, undoubtedly either not knowing or not thinking about my heritage, said,

"Wow! This must've been what it was like being an Indian around here." I might've laughed and asked for whatever it was he was smoking. I didn't tell him what crossed my mind, what I thought about the place just a stone's throw from the beach, where the old folks gathered herbs for colds and asthma. Or how half a mile north of the beach a jealous man murdered my grandmother's aunt and left her under a thicket of willow. Or how, during the late 1920s and '30s, first-generation Filipino men fought roosters under the bridge and, in their pinstriped suits and swinging their glinting gold watch chains, flirted with Indian girls, hoping for a wife. My grandmother said the bonfires were so big you could see the illuminated tops of the tall trees from across the river.

Much has changed here. The river is deep and still in the summer. The water, a putrid green, is unhealthy. "No Trespassing" signs line property on both banks. But the trees are still there. The county maintains a small regional park and has placed picnic tables under the redwoods and provided a lot where seasonal visitors pay a fee for parking. Seated at a table, I let my mind wander. Had I always been able to hear cars passing over the bridge? I couldn't remember being able to see the river from inside the trees, like I could now. What had changed? Was it the park visitors—now a couple walking their dog—that distracted me? Memories appeared and fled. I thought of looking for pitch, maybe on one of the tree trunks or perhaps oozing from a broken branch; the woman hadn't said where to look. Her babbling about love medicine felt remote now. Why had I taken time to come here? Any sense of urgency that I'd felt hearing her talk, and even the sense of urgency and awe these trees might inspire, escaped me. This grove couldn't have been where she'd come with her aunt to learn about love medicine.

I walked to the road and onto the bridge, where I could look down on the dirty water. I remembered the warm sand, the shallow, clear river. Talk of redwood trees and the river reminded me of those carefree days. I watched a pair of sparrows dart back and forth above the water. I didn't see an osprey, but maybe I just hadn't waited long enough.

Prior to the gold rush era, the coast redwoods covered a range of over two million acres. Today, only 5 percent of those ancient forests remain. Extensive logging of redwoods began in 1850, and mills soon sprung up throughout the region, located near railroads and waterways built to facilitate transportation of the wood to burgeoning San Francisco. In the 1840s, Stephen Smith, a sea captain and entrepreneur from Boston, had opened the first steam-generated mill in the town of Bodega, where, after marrying fifteen-year-old Peruvian Manuela Torres for the purpose of obtaining a Mexican land grant, he fathered three legitimate children as well as several more with his maid, a Coast Miwok woman named Tsupu and baptized

Maria Checca, my great-great-great-grandmother.

As the redwoods suffered and fell, so did the indigenous people. In 1850, vagrancy laws and indentured servitude, both utilized by the Mexican rancheros, were incorporated into one of California's first legislative measures, the Act for the Government and Protection of Indians, which legalized Indian slavery and remained in effect until 1868, three years after the end of the Civil War. According to the law of the land, stealing a white man's Indian was tantamount to stealing his horse.

Spanish laws imposed on natives sought not only to restrict their freedom and their use of the land (as with the prohibition on controlled burning) but also to take power over how they managed themselves. One rule said natives could not bathe at will in the missions; offended by their nudity, the Spanish padres permitted only an occasional bath with a bucket of water. Our people, cloaked in European clothes and unable to sweat and bathe in the traditional ways, became even more susceptible to European diseases to which we had no immunity, and pneumonia, smallpox, and syphilis ravaged mission populations and spread to unconquered villages. Conservative estimates suggest twenty thousand Coast Miwok and Southern Pomo inhabited present-day Marin County and the southern part of Sonoma County at the time of European contact. Today, more than two centuries later, of the fourteen hundred enrolled members of the Federated Indians of Graton Rancheria, all descend from among fourteen survivors from the original population. The survival rate was then, and is still, lower than that of the ancient redwoods, which also suffered at the hands of these same people.

As the trees disappeared, so did the forests' flora and fauna. Without cover of the dark woods, the most powerful creatures of the land, the grizzly bears, were vulnerable to farmers anxious to kill them to protect their livestock. Vaquero culture, which grew out of the Mexican rancho period, made sport of killing the huge creatures, lassoing them from horseback before shooting them, and many Americans adopted this practice. Arenas were built wherein, for the entertainment of settlers, captured bears were pitted against longhorn bulls in a fight to the death. The arenas' fences were made of the most durable lumber—redwood.

In the absence of redwood shade, mushrooms and mosses, exposed to direct sun, dried up, and redwood sorrel and redwood orchids, trillium and fairy bells, disappeared. Native foods such as huckleberries and several varieties of clover, also dependent on the forests' shade, became harder to find. Acorns, a staple of the California Indian diet, were also endangered, as tanoaks, on which grow the acorns most suitable for mush and bread, were no longer able to thrive in redwood clearings. The loss of tanoak groves also put the remaining redwoods in danger, as the smaller trees serve as buffers against fierce coastal winds and rains that can fell the towering giants;

redwoods have a shallow root system and no taproot to anchor them, and the most frequent cause of death, next to logging, is windthrow. Salmon, another principal food source, and an important part of the larger ecosystem, have also been affected by threats to the redwoods. When the land is in balance, fish spawn in streams that flow uninterrupted under the trees, and when the fish die after spawning, their decaying bodies provide important nutrients to the trees. When the trees are cut, this cycle is broken. Sediment from logged hillsides clogs the streams, and succeeding generations of salmon cannot navigate their way to spawn. The fish disappear. The people don't eat. Second-growth trees don't eat.

In the face of these changes, surviving natives adopted the settlers' diet. We learned to eat wheat and corn. With game scarce, we ate beef. What we wanted to do but couldn't was put things back in place. We couldn't open the grasslands for elk and pronghorn. We couldn't unclog the streams. The sedge beds where our mothers and grandmothers gathered roots for basket making, where were they? Where was the lake full of perch and catfish? Where did the redwoods go? Increasingly, we became strangers in our homeland. What happened to the outcropping of rocks that told the story of the greedy hunter? Isn't that wheat field where my grandfather's village was? No wonder the white man's religion began to make sense to some of us. Home isn't here, it's in the sky someplace.

The North Bay fire did not reach my home on Sonoma Mountain, but it came close. Driving down the mountain, after my neighbor's desperate 2 a.m. call to evacuate, I saw in the otherwise black night towering flames fifty feet from my car and, looking north to Santa Rosa, endless flames into the distance, an apocalyptic inferno. On the east side of the mountain, above the town of Glen Ellen, young, hand-planted redwood trees burned along with other trees caught in the fire. Within the last fifty years, developers have lined neighborhood thoroughfares and freeways with redwood trees, and homeowners have planted them in their backyards. Without the support of ancient giants that would, in a natural setting, grow alongside them, however, and without the requisite amount of fog that supplies 40 percent of a coast redwood's moisture, it remains to be seen if these inland trees will reach adulthood. (And that's not to mention what will happen if climate change affects the amount of fog redwoods will receive even when growing in their current range.) Can a young redwood tree withstand fire the way an older one can? A redwood's life span is two thousand years. A fifty-year-old tree is an infant.

The oldest redwood trees in Sonoma County live in Armstrong Redwoods State Reserve. One tree is fourteen hundred years old, another 310 feet high. Today the eight-hundred-acre reserve features picnic facilities, an outdoor amphitheater, and self-guided nature trails, but the main attraction is the ancient redwood grove, which the park's webpage notes is "a living reminder of the magnificent primeval redwood forest that covered much of this area before logging operations began during the nineteenth century." According to the website, "Colonel James Armstrong, an early-day lumberman, recognized the beauty and natural value of the forests he harvested [and] set aside the area as a 'natural park and botanical garden.'" But of course he hadn't "discovered" this natural wonder; local natives had lived beside it for centuries. Why hadn't I thought of *these* trees when I was told about love medicine?

Not long after the fire, I drove to Armstrong State Reserve, just outside of Guerneville, on the Russian River. More and more, I'd been thinking about love medicine, of the woman's mention of pitch from old trees. I wasn't interested in collecting the sap, or even seeing it—that is, if I was even able to find it. And anyway, I never did hear about the other necessary ingredients for the love medicine, and I'd long ago heeded Mabel McKay's advice to go about romance "the regular way." The main things on my mind were the recent fires and, to be honest, the assignment for this book. I had to write something. Go look at old redwoods, I told myself.

It was late afternoon when I arrived, the autumn sun already low in the sky, the day still unseasonably warm. From the parking lot, the trees were magnificent indeed, towering above the blacktop and cars. Each trunk was the size of a dozen people huddled together. Wisps of poison ivy lined a path to the picnic tables, the autumn-red leaves like lights announcing the forest.

Inside the forest, seated at a picnic table, I watched as the narrow columns of light filtering through the trees changed color, orange to red-violet. I thought of the things I knew. Was I seeing in that interplay of light and forest a thread for my imagination? The darkening light had to be the color of redwood pitch. Here, in these trees, the last Pomo woman who knew the ingredients and song for love medicine had walked with her old aunt for the first time. Kiss my ass. Isn't that what she'd said to the husband who'd jilted her? When the whale was at the mouth of the Gualala River, did water cover the forest here? The sharp scent of redwoods, pungent in the warm air, reminded me of sand beside a clean river. As daylight waned, the trees seemed to grow taller. I wanted to feel myself grow even smaller beneath them. But that didn't happen. I contented myself with what I'd seen earlier in that interplay of light and forest, that long play of history, the interrelatedness of all things, what I had understood in a single color—the color of pitch from a redwood tree. I saw my place in that history. And there was one thing more.

Days later the weather changed. Fog returned. My house sits high enough on Sonoma Mountain so that, looking west from my kitchen window, I can see the fog covering the Santa Rosa plain to form an inland sea. On that morning, I could see the tops of the trees on the coastal hills poking above the fog.

That is how the trees must've looked as my ancestors watched the ocean recede. And then the woman was there, above the fog and smiling confidently, just as she had when she'd said goodbye to me from her front door, only now she was saying hello. I understood. She never taught me love medicine. Maybe never cared to. What she did do for me was enough. The trees. I couldn't forget.

GREG SARRIS *is serving his thirteenth consecutive term as chairman of the Federated Indians of Graton Rancheria. He grew up in Sonoma County, where his Coast Miwok and Southern Pomo ancestors lived among the redwoods since time immemorial.*

The Science of Giants
Meg Lowman

Seeing a living redwood in person can be a transformational experience for anyone lucky enough to have the opportunity. The United States is home to the world's tallest tree species, but because *Sequoia sempervirens* grows within only a narrow strip along the Pacific Coast, less than 10 percent of Americans have ever seen one up close. More people have climbed Mount Everest than have ascended into a redwood tree canopy. Recently I took a group of Midwestern college students to Muir Woods, outside of San Francisco, as part of their summer tree-climbing research internship. Their reactions to seeing those tall, iconic redwoods echoed those that have come down through hundreds of years of similar encounters. One student wrote, "Looking at the size of these trees and the magnitude of their trunks makes me realize how small I am in the world, and especially in the universe."

Another wistfully commented, "Without trees, what is there?"

Most visitors to Muir Woods will pass by the popular park display of a redwood "cookie"—the forester's term for a slice of trunk that allows us to see the rings of a tree's history. Estimates propose that this tree started life as a seedling in AD 909 and grew for almost a thousand years before ending up as an interpretive exhibit in a national monument. This tree was witness to century after century of Native American culture, followed by the current period of modernization, including the 1849 California gold rush, which brought the world to the redwood forests and ultimately led to the harvesting of many redwood groves. That a single tree could live for a dozen human lifetimes feels beyond the grasp of our human minds.

And how do they grow to be so large?

A team led by botanist Steve Sillett at Humboldt State University recently discovered that older trees actually produce wood at a greater rate than younger trees. (Similar studies by forest research ecologist Nate Stephenson and his colleagues at United States Geological Services confirmed a similar trend in other tree species, showing that 97 percent of trees grow faster as they age—quite different from mammal species, which decrease their growth rates as they mature.) Larger trees also have more foliage, which allows them to photosynthesize more and produce even more wood.

Redwoods are also incredibly resourceful. They are, for instance, famously reliant on the moisture that characterizes the coastal region in which they grow, and they have developed an astoundingly efficient water transport system in order to make the most of the rainfall and fog they receive. The fact that water molecules can move from root hairs up through trunks and to the needles some hundreds of feet above ground is an amazing feat in and of itself, but even more incredible is how well the trees do it. Sillett's team discovered that part of what makes the tree's water transport system so efficient is the simple fact that redwood foliage is smaller and thicker in the canopy than in the understory, making it better equipped to endure the enormous tension created by the capillary action that draws water from the roots to the crowns.

The trees also regenerate themselves after they are damaged. Sillett, his tree-climbing research colleague Robert Van Pelt, and others have mapped the amazingly complex tree crowns of redwoods and discovered that these forest giants sprout new leaders in the upper canopy after wind or storms have damaged the existing boles. Such response to repeated weather conditions results in complex masses of leaders, both living and dead, along with massive amounts of detritus caught in the crotches, which then become home to entire communities of plant and animal life. A single redwood known as Iluvatar has been determined to have 220 trunks, comprising more than thirty-seven thousand cubic meters of wood. It is considered the most complex living organism on the planet. Epiphyte biologist Cameron Williams was once quoted as saying, "The top of Iluvatar is so dense with foliage that you could put on a pair of snowshoes and walk around on top and play Frisbee there."

If the size and complexity of a solitary redwood tree tests our ability to comprehend its existence, we must really stretch our senses to consider the timeline and historical range of the entire species. In geological nomenclature, redwoods are called "paleoendemics," meaning their current range represents only a remnant of the species' former distribution; the fossil record is our evidence of how widespread redwoods once were and how far back their existence can be traced. First recorded in the Mesozoic era some 150 to 200 million years ago, ancient redwoods had a nearly circumpolar arctic distribution as well as extensive distribution within the mid-latitude ranges—that is, they were also common throughout the western United States, Canada, Europe, Greenland, and China. As climates became cooler and drier almost 2 million years ago, during the Quaternary period, redwood distribution shrank to the current range along the coast of what is today central and northern California and southern Oregon. Once the American settlers moved west, the extensive logging practices of the nineteenth century reduced these old-growth forest fragments even further to approximately 113,000 precious acres.

To live for several thousand years—and survive as a species for millions of years—requires nearly miraculous levels of resilience, and the redwood may in fact be one of the most resilient organisms on the planet. The species has relatively few insect threats or deadly fungal pathogens, and, left alone, they tend to live a long, long time and grow to be enormous. Their main enemy is humans with chain saws; even forest fires do not threaten old-growth stands but rejuvenate them, rarely leaving more damage than an innocuous scar on the exterior bark and lower branches. Climate change may ultimately test the species' endurance, but only time will tell how these forest giants may adapt to more frequent drought and rising temperatures.

As iconic as redwood trees are, however, they may also be one of the least understood and least studied forest species on the planet. Today, the remnant stands of redwoods and the scientific knowledge we have about them remain almost as mysterious as the trees' mist-enshrouded canopies, but new technologies—including canopy-access techniques, aerial surveillance, and genetic tools—continue to advance our understanding of these giants. This essay highlights what we currently know about the redwoods, followed by sections on some of the more recent technologies that are enhancing redwood science and that will, ultimately, help future generations of redwood forest scientists conserve these majestic stands.

WET AND WILD

Before delving into the ways in which modern techniques and technology are changing our methods of studying the trees, we must first understand the questions driving such research. In fact, one of the most important elements of scientific research is asking the right questions. Today, one of the most valuable questions forest scientists are asking is, What specific environmental conditions allow redwoods to grow to such extraordinary heights and to survive for so long? The follow-up to that question is, naturally, to speculate how changes in our climate might affect the future of these great trees.

In looking at all the usual suspects—light, soil, moisture—scientists have identified a number of elements that support thriving redwood forests. For anyone who has spent time on the Pacific Coast, it might not come as a surprise that one of the most essential ingredients for Mother Nature's "secret recipe" for growing the tallest tree species in the world is fog. Biologist Todd Dawson and his active laboratory of students at the University of California, Berkeley, have spent decades studying this climate event and its intimate relation to coast redwoods, and they have found a strong correlation between redwood distribution and the fog that enshrouds the narrow strip of California coast during the otherwise dry summer months.

For the last several million years, coastal California has

experienced a Mediterranean-type climate, with cool, wet winters of adequate rainfall alternating with dry summers. It is during the summer months that the upwelling of cold ocean waters creates fog banks that blanket the coast and support the forests unique to this region. As the fog rolls in and is intercepted by the tall redwoods, water drips through the foliage to the forest floor and the soil, where it accounts for as much as a third of the forest's annual hydrologic input (defined as moisture from fog plus precipitation). Even more, in addition to providing water supplies directly to the trees and surrounding flora, fog also reduces evaporation and thereby increases the water efficiency of the redwood trees and their neighboring vegetation; in short, the water that gets to the forest stays in the forest. And redwoods don't just take in their water supply from the ground up. Dawson's team has discovered that redwood foliage is also capable of absorbing fog droplets directly into needles in the treetops, thereby shortcutting the longer, more conventional journey of water from tree roots up through the tall trunks and into the canopy. Dawson's team calculated that, during the summer months, redwood needles get an average of 6 to 8 percent of their water directly from fog. We are fortunate to have scientists willing to climb hundreds of feet into the treetops to conduct such measurements.

Foggy days are truly an asset to redwood health, and they're equally critical to whole-forest health. Climate models that predict decreases in fog for the California coast represent an enormous threat not only to the future distribution and health of the trees but also to the various life forms and ecological systems they support. In measuring fog input along the California coast for many years, Dawson and his students have noted an overall decline in fog over the past six decades, and in areas that have already been logged, the lack of moisture from fog is already threatening the surviving vegetation.

Save the Redwoods League chief scientist Emily Burns, an iconic redwood biologist affectionately known as the Fern Lady, has monitored fern ecology in redwood forests for over a decade, and her body of work on these understory plants can tell us much about the redwoods. Her perspective is the bottom-up counterpart to the Dawson team's top-down research.

One of Burns's most important discoveries related to fog and plant health seems obvious and yet was never previously documented: her research showed that the size and density of fern fronds reflect the climate in which they grow. Burns had spent hundreds of hours in the redwood forest before she finally came out with her theory; as she admits, she had to "see the forest for the ferns"—a good reminder that sometimes simple observations make for the best scientific discoveries.

After counting thousands of fronds, Burns recognized that the size and number of ferns in a redwood forest are indicators of forest moisture, whether from rainfall or fog. Sword ferns in drier forests south of San Francisco were dwarfs compared with their northern counterparts in moister forests closer to the

Oregon border. Simply put, the more rain and fog in the forest, the more ferns there were and the taller they grew. Burns now uses various redwood forests as climate-change laboratories, comparing the drier southern end of the redwood's range with the significantly wetter redwood forests up north. If moisture becomes scarcer over time, whether because of drought or loss of fog, ferns may very well shrink in the northern forests and become rare in the southern forests.

Burns has engaged a cadre of citizen scientists to monitor the fate of ferns in redwood forest understories, and her volunteers perform an annual checkup by counting sword ferns in twelve redwood forests as part of a Save the Redwoods League project called Fern Watch. While most redwood forest visitors spend their time gazing upward into the glorious canopy, the intrepid Fern Watch volunteers keep their focus underfoot, meticulously noting changes in fern height and density, and watching for any signs of drought stress, such as wilting or dying fronds or an increase in insects nibbling on the foliage. Although ferns are biologically renowned for producing toxins that normally deter insect defoliation, a stressed plant may not have the energy to produce such defenses, offering the insects a veritable banquet.

Between 2013 and 2017, the drought in California undeniably left its fingerprint on the sword ferns of the state's redwood forests: Fern Watchers observed that, as expected, the plants grew fewer and smaller fronds than in the years before the drought. With the return of heavy rains in 2017, Burns expects the ferns to respond by growing larger fronds and more of them, but no one can be sure given the rapidity with which climate change is altering ecological systems that have otherwise persisted for millennia. Whereas the cycle of greater lushness in times of surplus rain and fading vigor in times of drought has no doubt played out among the ferns for thousands, if not millions, of years, today we are encountering novel and more extreme environmental conditions, and the result might be that fern lushness fluctuates more dramatically or declines more noticeably in the decades ahead. We'll have to wait and see.

LIFE AT THE TOP

Back in the mid-1800s, Charles Darwin estimated that approximately eight hundred thousand species inhabited Earth—a number based entirely on ground-level observations. Just over one hundred years later, Terry Erwin, a biologist at the Smithsonian Institution, used insecticide to fog tropical tree canopies in Panama, then classified and counted the resultant rain of insects, and thereby raised Darwin's tally over fortyfold with an estimation that the planet was home to over thirty million insects alone. Almost one hundred and fifty years after Darwin, another iconic biologist, Professor E. O. Wilson at Harvard University, claimed that well over one hundred million species may exist on Earth, if we account not only for the treetop dwellers but for the soil microbes and deep-ocean inhabitants. He affectionately referred to the treetops as "the eighth continent." What these scientists confirm is that many species go unnoticed if we count only what we see at eye level. This is true for Earth as a whole, and it is also true for redwoods, which support a vast array of life forms from roots to treetops.

In the mid-twentieth century, scientists began to document the biodiversity of redwoods; but without the aid of modern canopy-access techniques, their observations were limited. Even so, their ground-based studies uncovered amazing information about the various life forms inhabiting these tall trees. The fauna of redwood forests, not surprisingly, appears to reflect an ecosystem that has remained relatively stable over recent millennia, with a variety of wildlife adapted to moist and shady habitats ranging from the woody debris of the forest floor to the emergent tree crowns exposed to full sunlight and extreme winds. That said, the lack of any comprehensive biological surveys several hundred years ago makes it impossible to accurately pinpoint what species may have gone extinct during the redwoods' lifetime. Even so, from the shaggiest bear to the most delicate damselflies, the biodiversity of a redwood forest may put Darwin's numbers to shame. Looking at just invertebrates alone, biologists who study what E. O. Wilson once called "the small things that run the world" have tallied more than eight thousand species of arthropods in redwood forests, including a healthy diversity of mites, millipedes, beetles, moths, silverfish, harvestmen, isopods, flies, crickets, centipedes, and a few butterflies. In 1990, entomologist Andrew Moldenke of Oregon State University recorded more than two hundred thousand orabatid mites representing seventy-five species living together on one square meter of redwood forest floor! In the plant world, Steve Sillett, working with epiphyte expert Cameron Williams in 2007, found 282 species of epiphytes in nine redwood crowns, including 183 lichens, 50 bryophytes, and 49 vascular plants. These are record-breaking numbers for a temperate forest, and the epiphyte diversity of the redwood canopy exceeded that of all other North American temperate forests.

With the disappearance of some 95 percent of old-growth redwood forests due to human activities over the last century and a half, however, many species associated with redwood trees have undoubtedly become extinct or threatened. Modern scientists have determined that several species of fauna are currently endangered, including the fisher, the northern spotted owl, the marbled murrelet, the coho salmon, and the Humboldt marten, found nowhere else on Earth. It is impossible to know how many species were lost with the disappearance and destruction of old-growth redwood forests during the last century. Today we are fortunate that groups such as Save the

Redwoods League, the Pacific Forest Trust, the Sempervirens Fund, and the Peninsula Open Space Trust (POST) remain vigilant in their objective to conserve the forests and save the species that live in them.

Jack Dumbacher, curator of birds at the California Academy of Sciences, is one of several scientists who have spent years documenting the decline of spotted owls in old-growth redwood forests. One of the major factors threatening this endangered species is the invasion by its close cousin, the barred owl. In a controversial move to protect the endangered birds, the Fish and Wildlife Service made efforts to remove barred owls from old-growth redwoods in hopes of restoring dwindling populations of spotted owls, but it remains to be seen whether the spotted owl can recover from the double threat of the barred owl plus habitat loss due to human activities. Preliminary results indicate that spotted owl populations are returning to old-growth forests after barred owls are removed, but the jury is still out on whether this experiment will be considered a success. Meanwhile, similar problems have arisen in old-growth forests between the endangered marbled murrelet and predatory crow populations (who are in part attracted by humans leaving food scraps at their campsites and along trails), and aggressive conservation efforts have been made to protect the small seabird from extinction.

That said, healthy redwood forests continue to provide a supportive habitat for countless creatures, and modern research techniques help us learn more about them and what we can do to ensure their survival. Advanced canopy-access techniques led to the classification of the wandering salamander (*Aneides vagrans*) in 1998, and as recently as May 2017 scientists classified a new species of coastal forest dweller, Humboldt's flying squirrel (*Glaucomys oregonensis*), who serves to remind us that new discoveries await in these tall trees. (As with the endangered marten, this new species was named after Prussian naturalist and explorer Alexander von Humboldt [1769–1859], who probably walked through the very same redwood forests some two hundred years before, cataloging new species.)

As redwood trees have been known to support the life of many other living things, these various species also seem to repay the trees by not turning them into lunch. Compared with the number of plant-eating animals found in tall tropical forests, redwood habitats feel almost devoid of herbivores. In fact, almost no insects consume redwood foliage or bark, a characteristic almost entirely unique in the world of forest science, in which insects reputably manage to defoliate most species of trees at regular intervals. A few scientific observations have cited insect damage to redwoods—cone moths and rounded borers have attacked redwood cones and seeds; aphids, scales, mealybugs, and leaf beetles can nibble or suck foliage; bark beetles and twig borers go after twigs; tip moths snack on buds; and bears occasionally strip bark off trunks—

but the impact is relatively minimal.

Biologist Paul Fine at U.C. Berkeley is currently studying the chemical basis of redwood defense mechanisms (that is, the toxins that may be keeping pests at bay), and his research supports the claim that redwoods have an extremely low herbivory rate. His team's data show that in a two-month period, an average of only 1 percent of the needle surface area of a redwood is eaten, as compared to 2 percent for the Douglas fir, which is second in line on the scale of low defoliation. The number for some tropical trees is a whopping 15 to 25 percent of foliage consumption per year. Fine is currently working on a comprehensive review of what secondary compounds—chemicals produced as a by-product of specific metabolic processes—might be working to create the unique defense system for the redwood foliage. (One chemical produced in redwoods is known to cause spontaneous abortion in cows!) What does this mean for redwoods? No one knows, but perhaps their impressive methods of self-defense will unlock even more secrets about their incredible resilience.

While redwoods are inhospitable to creatures who want to eat them, they are more than welcoming when it comes to animals and plants who want to call the trees home. Scientists now believe that almost half of Earth's creatures live in the canopy layers of various forests, and redwood biodiversity is an excellent example of the communities that thrive above our heads. Most trees produce a veritable "salad bar in the sky" for millions of insects, which are in turn eaten by myriad reptiles, amphibians, birds, and mammals, who themselves are then consumed by predators higher up the food chain. When they are not busy becoming someone's lunch, specialized insects and birds also participate in the complex canopy ecosystem by pollinating its thousands of flowering trees, vines, and epiphytes, and the chain continues on down to the ground, where the cycle of life is completed by soil decomposers (worms, fungi, and bacteria) breaking down and recycling organic matter back into the roots that feed the canopy.

Not surprisingly, as the atmospheric conditions vary along the length of a redwood, so do the plants and animals that call these microhabitats home. Both light and moisture are extremely variable from the top to the bottom of these forest stands; it is estimated that the light level reaching the floor of a redwood forest is only about 1 percent of the level hitting the treetops, creating many individual mini-ecosystems for a host of flora and fauna with different biological needs. The plant life alone is astoundingly diverse; biodiversity surveys have found over three hundred species of fungi and approximately one hundred lichens in just the canopy layer of redwoods, and it is likely those numbers underestimate what really exists in the old-growth treetops. Redwoods also host a long list of epiphytes—plants that live on the surfaces of other plants and derive their nutrition wholly from air and rainfall—including not just the conventional "air plants" like lichens and mosses but also ferns (the leather-leaf and licorice ferns), shrubs (huckleberry, trailing black currant, hairy manzanita, and salal), and sometimes small trees (tanoak, California bay laurel, Sitka spruce, and Douglas fir). Redwoods will even sprout on other redwoods, the young seedlings growing atop their giant relatives. In some cases, epiphyte growth isn't just the occasional sprout here and there, with the piggybacking plants having little to no effect on the host tree itself. Some of the fern mats are extremely dense (one tree boasted a grouping of over two thousand fronds), and when these epiphytes become heavy with moisture from rain and fog, they can either serve as an important source of water for other canopy inhabitants or cause branches to break under the extra weight and fall to the ground, where they become part of the ecosystem of the forest floor. This cycle has persisted for millions of years and will, hopefully, continue for millions more.

ADVANCES IN THE REDWOOD RESEARCH TOOLKIT

In light of recent developments in the fields of climate change and species extinction, researchers have looked to redwoods, and specifically to their canopies, as the proverbial "canary in the coal mine," with their health considered a harbinger of environmental change on a global scale. Today's forest scientists represent a new breed of planetary detective, seeking to unravel the critical mysteries of how forests function, in part for what they may tell us about Earth as a whole.

As iconic as redwoods have been to the humans fortunate enough to have seen them, they have remained mysterious in part because one of the features that makes them so impressive also makes them inaccessible. Canopy exploration is a relatively recent field of study in part because climbing three-hundred-plus feet up a trunk is no proverbial walk in the park. Humans developed SCUBA gear in the 1950s and visited the moon in the 1960s, but field biologists (including myself) did not explore the tops of any forest trees with a deliberate and repeatable methodology until the early 1980s. Very few people have climbed into a redwood crown, and to this day the canopies of these giants remain one of the least-explored parts of our planet.

Early canopy-access techniques used equipment adapted from cave exploration, and progress of this technology into more precise and efficient research tools has completely transformed the science of these forest giants. What started out as using a slingshot to propel a rope over a canopy branch has developed into expanded technologies that borrow from both mountaineering and cave exploration and that take advantage of developments in modern materials. No longer limited to movement up and down a rope, today's forest scientists can transition horizontally between different crowns and use inflatable devices such as canopy rafts anchored in the treetops to extend their stays and collect data.

As one of the pioneers of the field, botanist Steve Sillett, now in his third decade of forest research, has continued to make new discoveries about the higher reaches of giant trees, including redwoods. Sillett's students and cohorts became the first scientists to document biodiversity in the upper reaches of redwood crowns, and his work in the area of canopy plant life has yielded a wealth of information. Others working to advance canopy research include epiphyte biologist Cameron Williams and lichenologist Rikke Reese Næsborg (both of U.C. Berkeley, and also husband and wife), who together, with funding from Save the Redwoods League, have studied how epiphyte communities vary along latitudinal gradients, and determined which factors (age of the tree, structure of the crown, moisture, and light) impact the success of epiphytes in redwood crowns. Modern technology combined with their tenacity to climb more than two hundred feet into the tops of redwoods have opened a new chapter in redwood science. In a popular article about her work, Næsborg was quoted as saying, "We really don't know what we'd be missing if we don't climb the trees." Just as this book went to press, Næsborg published a new species of lichen she had found in the redwood canopies thanks to access provided by her ropes and climbing hardware.

Also helping expand the field of tree study is the development and use of digital camera technology. In their research over the past decade, a team of herpetologists led by Jim

Campbell-Spickler have employed camera surveillance to monitor the activity of the canopy-dwelling wandering salamander (*Aneides vagrans*). First discovered in a canopy treehole of a fallen trunk by Hartwell Welsh in 1995, this salamander was notable for being the first species known to live its entire life in the treetops rather than on the forest floor—a lifestyle aided by its long limbs and prehensile tail.

Another canopy-access tool used in the field these days is the type of crane you might expect to see only on a construction site. As part of a team with Dave Shaw, Kristine Ernest, and Bruce Rinker in 2004, I spent several seasons working from the bucket of a construction crane measuring the insect damage to tall trees in Wind River, Oregon. The crane made it so much easier to return to our study area and make measurements than when we were using slingshots and a length of rope.

At the other end of the spectrum from enormous construction cranes are the high-powered, highly sensitive desktop microscopes, including scanning electron microscopes (SEM), that have allowed researchers to unlock the secrets of redwood forests by studying their smallest inhabitants. Some of the tiniest organisms on the planet—not only insects but also their even smaller counterparts, such as microscopic invertebrates—inhabit redwood canopies and are still relatively mysterious. In the summer of 2015, I co-led a team of students in wheelchairs (along with mobile students) with Professor

Randy Miller from Baker University, in Kansas, to climb trees and inspire mobility-limited students to experience field biology as a possible career choice. Our team analyzed samples collected in the redwood canopies to find tardigrades (commonly called water bears), a phylum of miniature aquatic invertebrate animals that share ancestry with arthropods and nematodes. Much to our amazement, every single sample of moss, lichen, or bark in the canopies of tall Pacific Northwest trees contained at least one tardigrade! These water-dwelling creatures live in moist environments ranging from marine and freshwater locations to tree bark crevices, moss, lichen, and foliage. Their unique ability to survive a wide range of conditions—enormous heat, cold, pressure, starvation, dehydration, and even radiation—has given these "extremotolerant" creatures a reputation as one of the toughest organisms in the world. (When they were launched into outer space, they not only survived but reproduced.) The redwoods represent ideal habitat for these microscopic critters, but before the existence of modern research tools and techniques, it was simply impossible to study them with any precision. In fact, no one ever sampled tardigrades in the redwoods until our expedition of undergraduates sampled micro-arthropod life in these tall trees. We also helped advance inclusivity in field biology by adapting available canopy-access techniques to our mobility-limited students. In a small way, including students who use wheelchairs in the field of canopy science will increase the diversity of perspectives that inevitably advance forest conservation.

Another nascent development in redwood research is the exploration of the species on a genetic level. Soon after forest-science pioneers began ascending into tree canopies, the field of molecular genetics expanded to allow greater insight into the biological lineages of various trees species and their relatives. So far the field has confirmed the common genetic profile of individual redwoods that are part of the same "fairy rings," or trunks sprouting in close proximity and often forming a circle, and genetic markers have also confirmed the creation of a single, or monophyletic, conifer lineage within the Cyprus family, *Cupressaceae*, which includes redwoods and other related species.

Recent advances in genetics are also providing insights into how we might conserve redwoods in the future, even as they challenge some earlier misguided preservation efforts. Traditional techniques of thinning and harvesting redwood forests, for instance, has been found in some cases to endanger the future of the trees, although not in the way one might think. Lakshmi Narayan at U.C. Berkeley studied coast redwood genetic clones at Big Basin Redwoods State Park, near Santa Cruz, and found, to her amazement, that genetic diversity was lowest in old-growth stands with a history of partial timber harvest. Her research showed that loggers, despite their best intentions to harvest trees conservatively and selectively by cutting just a few trees at a time, actually lowered the genetic diversity of redwoods because they were, unbeknownst to them, cutting genetically similar trees. The result is that the remaining population is less genetically diverse and therefore less adaptable to a variety of threats, including drought, increased atmospheric temperatures, disease, and pests. Today we know that it is only through explorations into the genetic information of the trees that forest managers and conservationists can select trees for harvest that will allow us to preserve the greatest genetic diversity to ultimately help the species survive.

Botanists Jean Langenheim and G. D. Hall have also used genetics to study the trees and their ability to adapt to different environments. Their team from U.C. Santa Cruz found that redwoods in the southernmost forests represented a different colonizing population, or provenance, from those in the northern and central California forests, and that, in each case, the local provenance grew better in its native environment than did transplanted individuals. This finding is important for conservation efforts because it confirms that successful restoration of logged forests is not as simple as merely bringing in outside seed sources to repopulate cleared areas.

New genomic techniques are also now allowing scientists to sequence conifer genomes, including the enormous redwood genome, which will open the door to learning even more about the trees' evolutionary makeup. The redwood genome has sixty-six chromosomes, compared to the human genome's forty-six and the twenty to twenty-four chromosomes of most conifers. This anomaly, called hexaploidy (meaning there are six copies of each chromosome), explains how these trees are capable of such enormous genetic variation. Coast redwoods are the only hexaploid conifer, which suggests there might have been hybridization among now-extinct redwood species during the time when their range was much broader.

Emily Burns at Save the Redwoods League, David Neale at U.C. Davis, and Steven Salzburg at Johns Hopkins University have partnered on the Redwood Genome Project to map the enormous redwood genome, the results of which will be applied to future redwood conservation management in order to protect genetic diversity for increased forest resilience. With the first complete reference genome sequence for the coast redwood made available in 2018, forest managers will be able to screen the genetic diversity of forests by sampling a few leaves or small sections of young bark from trees across the landscape. This new genome inventory information will identify both where natural diversity is high and worthy of enhanced protection and where restoration treatments to accelerate the growth of harvested forests needs to proceed carefully to prevent any further diversity loss. It cannot be overstated how critical the preservation of the genetic diversity of redwoods is for the future of the species.

As modern advances bring us ever closer to understanding our world, scientists never stop seeking new tools and technologies to enhance their research. Progress in canopy-access techniques and genomic analysis, for instance, still remain focused on individual one-tree-at-a-time research in most cases, but new developments will help expand that knowledge to include an ecological overview of entire stands and whole forests. One of the newest innovations is an aerial assessment method called lidar (an acronym based on the description "light detection and ranging"), which uses laser detection to re-create three-dimensional models of the areas being surveyed. The lidar method has been around since the early 1960s, but it continues to benefit from advances in related technology, among them a comprehensive approach called AToMS (Airborne Taxonomic Mapping System), which uses various integrated sensory tools in combination with a computing package to determine the species composition and defense mechanisms of the forests. Ecologist Greg Asner and his research team at Stanford University's Carnegie Institute have used this system in their pioneering lidar overflights of redwood forests (and other forests around the world), on which they have collected amazing levels of detail about the growth, carbon storage, drought impacts, and insect attacks of not just the tree crowns but also the understory or forest floor. These revolutionary technologies use laser imagery and sensitive cameras to detect various properties of the trees many thousands of feet below the tools themselves.

Rounding out the information collected through airborne

research techniques is a method called "ground-truthing," in which a team on the ground confirms (or adjusts) the data collected by the survey tools. Forest physiologist Anthony Ambrose and forest scientist Wendy Baxter climbed forty-nine enormous sequoia trees as part of the ground-truthing of the treetops for lidar overflights in California; and in the Amazon, Asner's teams have climbed seventy-five trees per day and compiled ground-truthed information on more than five thousand species as part of a mission to accurately interpret the health of tropical rain forests.

Save the Redwoods League funded the Carnegie team to conduct lidar mapping of Redwood National Park in 2007. The effort not only charted the trees but also collected information useful in, for instance, identifying potential mudslides that could choke streams and endanger salmon, as well as providing data to help manage stands for restoration by earmarking regions where young redwood regrowth was overly dense. Since then, airborne teams have also surveyed extensive regions of Northern California to monitor the impacts of drought. In 2015, the Carnegie team joined forces with the aerial team of CAL FIRE to assess losses in the water content of California forest canopies, which they did using laser-guided spectroscopy and satellite-based models. The results indicated an astounding number of dead crowns, and severe water loss of over 30 percent in at least one million hectares, comprising approximately fifty-eight million large trees. Fortunately, the drought conditions of 2012–15 were partially ameliorated by rainfall in 2016, although the recurrence of extreme drought is likely and will continue to stress the forests of California in the future.

The Carnegie lidar team is currently collaborating with another aerial group, called Planet Labs, which uses satellites to perform more nimble and frequent overflights of drought-stricken forests. Planet Labs will enable detection of rapid changes in the health of California's trees, including redwoods, in an effort that will, according to Asner, "vastly improve our scientific support for environmental conservation, management, and decision-making."

Research that combines redwood forest mapping with climate models are also increasing our understanding of climate change and how it might impact the redwood forests. Scientists have predicted that redwood habitat will become warmer over the next century, and a new program called the Redwoods and Climate Change Initiative (RCCI), also funded by Save the Redwoods League, has confirmed that individual redwood trees are actually growing bigger under recent warming trends, a fact that allows us some degree of optimism when considering the species' ability to adapt to climate change. RCCI is the most comprehensive and ambitious research project ever conducted on redwood trees, assembling the most comprehensive data set and analysis of growth rates, aboveground biomass, and stand dynamics ever compiled for one species of tree. All these efforts—from advances in canopy-access hardware to genomics and lidar mapping—not only provide important data about the present condition of redwoods but also offer clues about their future.

What's next? We look forward to the development of new field methods and laboratory equipment in our efforts to discover much more about the redwoods and the plants and animals that live alongside them. We are only just beginning.

For as much as we worry about the survival of the species—and we are right to do so—we also have decades of research proving what incredible survivors these trees are. They protect themselves from pests and fire, adapt to drought and heat, and regenerate themselves after being cut. These giants have existed on Earth for longer than we have, and some experts say there is no reason to suspect they won't outlive our own species. The key will be understanding what we can do to help protect them in the face of so many destructive human activities.

Redwood canopy scientist Cameron Williams says, "If more people were able to climb among the branches of such an immense living organism, I believe we'd have better conservation values as a whole." Perhaps soon, the extraordinary privilege of accessing a redwood crown will be available to more than just a handful of daring scientists. As part of its centennial celebration, Save the Redwoods League is planning a canopy-access exhibit in Northern California to educate both citizens and landowners alike. The Sequoia Zoo in Eureka, California, and the Yurok tribe of Northern California are also exploring ways to share the spiritual and biological magic of redwood canopies with a broader public, and the zoo is currently designing a canopy walkway adjacent to its current exhibits. Perhaps allowing the public to discover the wonders of Mother Nature from atop a giant redwood tree instead of just from its base will inspire a new generation of explorers and conservationists. For the redwoods to become a lasting legacy for future generations, we need to keep learning from the trees, listening to the lessons they can teach us about adaptability and survival, resistance and resilience—all increasingly important attributes for any species in a changing environment. With luck, they will teach us not only about themselves but also about ourselves.

MEG LOWMAN *is one of the world's pioneers in canopy research and passionately pursues forest conservation and inspiring women and girls in science. Her research has ranged from microscopic water bears living on the canopy of tall dipterocarp trees in Malaysia to sloths and bromeliads in the treetops of the Amazon rain forests. But she admittedly harbors enormous respect for the heights of redwoods and those who climb these* *forest giants. She is a senior scientist and the Lindsay Chair of Botany at the California Academy of Sciences, when she is not climbing a tree somewhere in a remote jungle.*

The author extends a giant redwood-sized thanks to the staff at Save the Redwoods League, and especially Emily Burns, for assistance with archival reports. Thanks also to the many folks who answered questions, provided scientific reprints, and shared their stories of redwood-love.

Redwood Time
David Rains Wallace

John C. Merriam taught paleontology at U.C. Berkeley from 1894 to 1920, and he was a leading field and research scientist. He excavated and described many California fossils, including the famous ice age mammals of the La Brea tar pits and much older marine reptiles from the Klamath Mountains. His profession (*paleontology* means "knowledge of old things") gave him special insight into living organisms as well as extinct ones, and a short essay on coast redwoods that he published in 1930 probably has done as much to protect the world's tallest trees as anything written about them. Titled "A Living Link in History," it helped to create a lasting constituency for the genus *Sequoia* by evoking not only the trees' beauty but their age:

As you advance into these splendid forests, an almost

infinite variety in expression of light and shade and color, and a perspective with marvelously changing depth, compose a scene such as canvas has yet to receive. . . . But woven through this picture is an element which eludes the imagery of art. . . . Living trees like these connect us as by hand-touch with all the centuries they have known. . . . It is as if in these trees the flow of years were held in eddies, and one could see together past and present. The element of time pervades the forest with an influence more subtle than light, but that to the mind is not less real.

The essay gets at what impresses us most about old-growth redwoods: the way their lives reach back through human history. Growing up in New England, I remember how intrigued I was when I saw a picture of a redwood trunk section with growth rings that showed it had been alive during the Roman Empire, two millennia ago. Yet Merriam's essay also brings up a problem with our perception of redwoods. The trunk that enthralled me as a child was easy to comprehend because it was sectioned and labeled. When I later saw a living redwood forest, I certainly was impressed, but the very fact of its monumental stability made the sight harder to grasp. The huge trees soared; ferns and mosses clustered below them; a Steller's jay might call. But that seemed to be about all that was happening there much of the time.

Along with evoking the forest's venerability, Merriam's essay also contributes to this sense of bafflement at its monumentality, a bafflement that California governor Ronald Reagan expressed—and then dismissed—when he asked: "How many trees do you need to see?" Part of the problem may be that the 1930 essay's leisurely style and tone of hushed reverence—"arches of foliage . . . beauty of light filling dark spaces"—can seem dated in the twenty-first century. But I think it goes deeper than that. Perhaps the root of the problem is that although Merriam's idea of forest time flowing in eddies that connect past and present seems right, an old-growth redwood stand has less *perceptible* time flow than most landscapes, so that experience of it can veer less toward intimations of time's "living currents" than of a kind of woody stasis.

Not that other writers have produced anything more influential than Merriam's essay, which helped in the creation of today's redwood state and national parks. After admiring the North Coast's redwoods when I first came to California in the 1960s, I veered inland and wrote about the less monolithic but more diverse mixed conifer-hardwood forests of the Klamath Mountains. I've since published about redwoods, including chapters of the *Redwood National Park Handbook*, but I've continued to feel a certain inadequacy. One magazine editor felt impelled to add an uplifting "how to" finale to a piece of mine about that park that must have seemed insufficiently inspirational: "Spend some time in solitary communion with the forest so you depart with a feeling of reverence and awe," he wrote. "This is nature's cathedral, where services are heard daily under the vaulted roof of the redwoods."

The closest I've come to what felt like a deep plunge into Merriam's sense of "redwood time" was when, backpacking in the Ventana Wilderness east of Big Sur, I encountered a small, ancient grove in a canyon just below where the Santa Lucia Mountains rise to their chaparral-covered crest. The redwoods there were broad, but short compared to those of the national park or even farther west in Big Sur, and the ground was not lush with ferns and mosses. The trees were facing ecological limits, and somehow their peripheral isolation made them seem more comprehensible than their bigger relatives, almost animate, like Tolkien's tree-like Ents. I could definitely feel "the flow of years . . . held in eddies."

The remote grove was easy to sleep in and I felt unusually energetic the next morning, as though immersion in redwood time could evoke an actual biological regeneration as well as "reverence and awe." The wilderness area's ancient dwarfs hinted at more than monumental grandeur tending to woody stasis. But how—aside from sleeping with redwoods—can a twenty-first-century mind, full of tweets and sound bites, get past the woody mass to the "living currents"? John Merriam's profession suggests one way. He was able to connect with redwoods in time as well as space because he knew a great deal about their past. And it is an impressive past.

LOST WORLDS

The coast redwood forests' woody mass seems to have overwhelmed the first European naturalists to see it in the late eighteenth century. Their descriptions stress size more than other qualities, as though they saw the trees mainly as obstacles. An expedition led by the American explorer Jedediah Smith in 1828 found redwood forest literally impassible on the journey to the Pacific from the Sacramento Valley. The party had to backtrack and follow rivers instead of going overland. With the rapid growth of evolutionary thinking in the mid-nineteenth century, however, naturalists became increasingly impressed with the redwoods' age, and not only that of individual living trees but of the genus. Early paleontologists began to find such a vast quantity of redwood fossils that they were literally stumbling over them. I've stumbled on them myself.

The Hellroaring Creek backcountry in Yellowstone National Park is a plateau of forest and meadow like many in the Mountain West, but I got a surprise there in 1978 when, fording a stream one day, I realized that the slippery cobbles in its bed were fossilized pieces of fibrous bark and straight-grained wood, like redwood fossils I'd seen in California. Years later, hiking the bluffs above the Lamar Valley in northeastern Yellowstone, I came on an entire rusty-gray fossil trunk looming among the living pines. A bison stood by it, so I didn't get close enough to examine the massive column, but it looked familiar, again like the fossilized redwood trunks I'd seen in California.

Many such fossil trunks stand in Yellowstone. Jim Bridger, a fur trapper who saw them in the early 1800s, was said to have been so intrigued that he embroidered his account with tall tales of fossil birds singing "petrified" songs on fossil branches. Because of such wonders, Congress made this remote volcanic plateau the first national park in 1872. The wonders also made it a prototype for a whole genre of paleontologically oriented science fiction thrillers, first represented by Arthur Conan Doyle's classic *The Lost World*, about a remote South American plateau inhabited by dinosaurs and other prehistoric giants.

As it happened, redwood fossils figured as important evidence of other "lost worlds" during the park's first year. Asa Gray, Harvard University's first botany professor and an associate of Charles Darwin, was one of the first naturalists to study plants of the past as well as the present. Addressing an 1872 meeting of the American Association for the Advancement of Science, he noted that "Sequoia and its Relatives" comprise a group with similar forms living in widely separate parts of the Northern Hemisphere, and that, since such similarities arise from common inheritance, this suggests that sequoia and its relatives must be a very old group. "The needful facts," Gray went on in reference to that great age, "have now been for some years made known." Citing fossils found in millions-of-years-old Miocene-epoch rock strata of northern Europe, he noted that fossils from the same *Sequoia* species were "abundantly found" in similarly aged deposits of Iceland, Greenland, Canada, and Alaska: "It is named *S. langsdorfii*, but it is pronounced to be very much like *S. sempervirens*, our living redwood of the California coast, and to be an ancient representative of it." He added: "Fossil specimens of a similar, if not the same, species have recently been detected in the Rocky Mountains . . . [and] another Sequoia (*S. sternbergii*), discovered in Miocene deposits in Greenland, is pronounced to be the representative of *S. gigantea*, the big tree of the California Sierra."

Gray didn't spell out the implication of his "needful facts," but it clearly was that the sequoia and its relatives probably came into existence not through what was traditionally known as divine creation but through what Darwin was then calling "descent with modification," now known as evolution. "I think we may, with our present light, fairly assume," Gray discreetly concluded, "that the two redwoods of California are the direct or collateral descendants of the two ancient species which so closely resemble them. . . . So the Sequoias . . . are of an ancient stock [and] their ancestors and kindred formed a large part of the forest which flourished throughout the polar regions, now desolate and ice-clad, and which extended into the low latitudes in Europe."

Redwood time may seem like woody stasis now, but it has

"flowed" over a lot more of the earth than its present distribution might suggest. A jetliner can cross *Sequoia sempervirens*'s existing range in an hour or two now; it would have taken a day or more to overfly the vast forests of the tree's ancestors. Redwood time reaches back not just through human history but through a prehistory that has confounded long-held beliefs. The "living currents" are almost unimaginably deep: lost worlds indeed.

TIME CLAIMS

Gray's address didn't expound further on the redwood fossils "recently detected in the Rocky Mountains," but that probably was because his audience already knew about them. Their "detector," Ferdinand V. Hayden, was a celebrity, a geologist who began exploring the West in the 1850s, and who in 1871 and 1872 led U.S. government expeditions that promoted Yellowstone as a park. Scientific explorers like him were major players in an enterprise that involved "the winning of the West" and that would have greater implications for ideas about the future of civilization. The ranchers and miners who followed geological surveys like Hayden's onto the Great Plains and into the Rockies after the Civil War were winning space, an old part of civilization's drive to escape socioeconomic stasis through geographic expansion. The geologists were "winning" time, a newer, more problematic enterprise.

Could geological time be "won" as ranchers and miners won geographic space? The question seems metaphysical. But paleontological "bone barons" like Edward D. Cope and Othniel C. Marsh had begun acting as though they could win parts of time, staking claims on western fossil deposits, pitting digger crews against each other in "bone rushes," and exchanging accusations of time theft and time fraud in newspaper scandals. And their claims paid off as they negotiated their collections into academic positions, government jobs, and international reputations. In their louche way, the boxing bone barons addressed the same vital issue as genteel Asa Gray in his sequoia address. Marsh, a Yale professor, used his fossils to promote Darwin's "descent with modification"; Cope, a wealthy virtuoso, used his to promote less materialistic ideas of "transmutation" through "inheritance of acquired traits."

Time claims involved more than scientific theories and reputations. They raised the question as to who should claim time—and for what? Should barons able to buy it and sequester it in their "cabinets" be the chief claimants? Or should the public have a stake? The public had growing reasons for wanting one. The idea that titanic geological forces had shaped the earth while giants ruled it over millions of years captured the popular imagination, and not only in the emerging mass media's sensationalist way. It evoked feelings that bordered on the numinous. One of Cope's bone diggers, Charles H. Sternberg, recalled in his memoirs that when his boss, a lapsed but still religious Quaker, spoke of the fossil past, "so absorbed did he become on his subject that he talked on as if to himself . . . while I listened entranced."

Of course, religions have always owned sacred times. Could vast epochs ruled by monsters be sacred? Sternberg had begun to think so. Finding fossil wood and leaves beneath the Kansas prairie, he exulted: "Go back with me, dear reader, and see the treeless plains of to-day covered with forests. . . . We can imagine that the Creator walked among the trees in the cool of the evening . . . but the glorious picture is only for him who gathers the remains of these forests, and by the power of his imagination puts life into them."

Yellowstone National Park was a response to the question of time ownership. The park's advocates saw it not only as a "pleasuring ground" but as a stage for the presentation of a new, geological "creation myth" of unprecedented grandeur and venerability—a recreational adventure in time as well as space. In his 1901 book *Our National Parks*, pioneer conservationist John Muir urged Yellowstone visitors to "take a look into a few of the tertiary volumes of the grand geological library of the park, and see how God writes history."

Hayden and his colleagues had an even more intriguing account of the park's fossil redwoods than the old trapper's "petrified" birdsongs. They surmised that volcanic eruptions had buried living forests in hot ash during repeated catastrophic events many millions of years ago, accounting for the fossils' still-standing positions. Geologists eventually identified twenty-seven such petrified redwood forests that eruptions had repeatedly buried over a period of twenty thousand years, when Yellowstone was a land of low hills and wide valleys with a climate like present-day Florida's. It was a world both strange and familiar, where now extinct giant mammals—ursine creodonts, bovine coryphodons—lived with ancestral redwoods in forests that also held ancestors of the park's living bears, bison, and cottonwood trees.

A CENTURY OF PROGRESS

The Yellowstone fossils' strange-familiar lost world raised questions about time's nature. Uniform geological processes like volcanoes and erosion made time seem cyclic, always the same as mountains arose and wore away. But did a mix of extinct and extant life forms in a fossil deposit mean that time is "going somewhere"? The only sign of such "progress" that earlier paleontologists like Richard Owen and Charles Lyell had recognized—humanity's late appearance in the fossil record—seemed to imply divine intervention rather than natural processes. Lyell, called "the father of geology" because of his pioneering analyses of the fossil record, suspected that nonhuman biology might be as uniformly cyclic as geology, and that climatic changes might bring back extinct life forms as geological ones revive eroded mountains: "The huge iguanodon might reappear in the woods, and the ichthyosaur in the sea, while the pterodactyl might flit again through the umbrageous groves of tree ferns."

Lyell could equally have mentioned "umbrageous groves" of redwoods, because paleontologists began finding fossil sequoias that resembled living specimens not only in the strange-familiar, mammal-dominated deposits of what he named the Tertiary period but also in the even stranger ones of the previous Cretaceous and Jurassic periods, when reptilian giants that Owen named dinosaurs ("terrible lizards") held sway. Sixty-foot sauropods seemed an even better match for three-hundred-foot redwoods than ten-foot mammoths. If a future warming climate might allow redwoods to reclaim the Arctic, who could say that saurian giants might not return to browse in their groves?

The nineteenth century was the Century of Progress, however. Although few fossil signs of successive change were known early in the 1800s, more emerged as collections grew. When Cope and Marsh explored Tertiary deposits in the 1870s and '80s, they found different mammal faunas in every epoch, and although their interpretations of change differed, both men stressed improvement as a primary feature. Marsh measured the brain cavities of successive mammal species and found progressive enlargement leading to "survival of the fittest." Cope thought mammals were getting smarter by passing "acquired traits" to their descendants.

There were limits to their upwardly mobile interpretations, however. Fossils showed that the dinosaur age had lasted much longer than the age of mammals, yet dinosaurs showed little sign of cumulative mental improvement. Many plants had changed hardly at all during and after the dinosaur age. In his 1872 address, Asa Gray noted that European Cretaceous deposits had yielded a fossil cone "like that of *Sequoia gigantea* in its famous groves," and that Cretaceous deposits in Greenland had yielded "two more Sequoias, one of them identical with the Tertiary species, and one nearly allied to *Sequoia langsdorfii*, which in turn is a probable ancestor of the common California redwood."

Plant life had changed overall in the late dinosaur age as flowering trees came to dominate Northern Hemisphere temperate forests with what Gray called the "Arcto-Tertiary flora"—the northern Age of Mammals flora. French paleontologist Gaston de Saporta had a progressive interpretation of this change, theorizing that early angiosperms had "coevolved" with fruit-and-seed-eating early mammals to develop more-nutritious fruits and seeds, which in turn had caused mammals to get larger, evolve larger brains, and increasingly compete with dinosaurs. Darwin was skeptical of this theory, calling angiosperm origins "an abominable mystery," but progress-minded naturalists like Gray saw no necessary discrepancy between slowly changing plants and a progressively evolving world. Summing up his 1872 address, he declared:

> Organic Nature—by which I mean the system and totality of living things, and their adaptation to each other and to the world—with all its apparent and indeed real stability, should be likened not to the ocean, which varies only by tidal oscillations from a fixed level to which it is always returning, but rather to a river, so vast that we can neither discern its shores nor reach its sources, whose onward flow is not less actual because [it is] too slow to be observed by the ephemerae which hover over its surface.

MIRACULOUS VIRTUES

Progressive optimists regarded public time claims like Yellowstone as harbingers of socioeconomic improvement as well as shrines to a splendid past. Another early fur trapper, Joe Meek, likened the plateau's geyser basins to "the industrial city of Pittsburgh." John Muir, a farmer, inventor, and industrial efficiency expert as well as a conservationist and naturalist, described the park's Midway Geyser Basin similarly: "These valleys at the heads of the great rivers may be regarded as laboratories or kitchens in which, amid a thousand retorts and pots, we may see Nature at work as a chemist."

Influenced by the new ways of thinking about life in time, Muir saw a similar practical role for the Sierra Nevada's giant sequoias. Historians had noted how ancient civilizations' destruction of forests for fuel and construction caused streams to flood disastrously or dry up because the trees no longer protected the soil from erosion, which then contributed to socioeconomic declines. Linking this history to logging in the Sierra Nevada, Muir advocated the giant sequoia as "a tree of life to the dwellers of the plain dependent on irrigation, a never-failing spring, sending living waters to the lowland. For every grove cut down a stream is dried up. Therefore, all of California is crying 'Save the trees of the fountains.'"

Yet Muir distrusted using Darwinian evolution to justify rampant socioeconomic growth, as many progressives began to do. The idea that natural selection had operated mechanically over indifferent eons seemed soulless, and the assumption held by quarrelsome scientists like Cope and Marsh that primeval savagery had dominated those eons was repugnant: "We gaze morbidly through civilized fog upon our beautiful world . . . and see ferocious beasts and wastes. . . . We deprecate bears. But grandly they blend with their native mountains." Muir saw wild nature as essentially beyond ownership—measureless, timeless. "[A bear's] life not long, not short, knows no beginning, no ending. To him life unstinted, unplanned, is above the accidents of time, and his years, markless and boundless, equal Eternity."

Muir liked to meditate on fossil forests but showed less interest in fossil monsters, although he did liken the giant sequoia to one, writing that it looked "as strange in aspect and behavior among its neighbor trees as would the mastodon among the honey bears and deer." He saw evolution as cooperation more than competition, and he wanted to preserve wild nature for pantheist religious reasons more than socioeconomic ones: "No wonder that so many fine myths have originated in springs; that so many fountains were held sacred in the youth of the world, and had miraculous virtues ascribed to them." He saw the Sierra's fountain-generating sequoias as ultimate exemplars of such virtues: "So exquisitely harmonious and finely balanced are even the very mightiest of these monarchs of the woods in all their proportions and circumstances there never is anything overgrown or monstrous-looking about them. . . . Walk the Sequoia woods at any time of year and you will say that they are the most beautiful and majestic on earth."

I suspect that giant sequoias' distribution—scattered through the Sierra in relatively small, open, and walkable groves—contributed to Muir's enthusiasm for what is now named *Sequoiadendron giganteum*. When I first saw a sequoia grove, in Yosemite, it reminded me of the Ent-like coast redwoods in the Ventana Wilderness more than the dense coastal groves farther north. In contrast to the Sierra, his "range of light," the shadowy North Coast seems to have daunted Muir rather as it did earlier explorers, although he reached California too late to see its forest whole. San Francisco already was built from coast redwood when he arrived in 1867. But that was another reason why he was determined to keep the Sierra's sequoias safe. In a posthumously published journal, he writes: "Had not the Sierra forests grown at high altitude and thus been rendered difficult of access, they would all have been felled ere this. Meanwhile the redwood of the Coast and the Douglas spruce of Washington and Oregon were more available. . . . The trees pressed close to the shores as if courting their fate . . . while the redwoods filled the river valleys, opening into bays forming good harbors for ships." He also notes that while giant sequoia wood is too brittle for most commercial uses, coast redwood is not.

Redwoods in the pre–gold rush Oakland Hills had been so tall that ships used them as landmarks when sailing into San Francisco Bay. In 1886, Muir and an Alameda physician named Gibbons took the English naturalist Alfred Russell Wallace, famous as Darwin's "co-discoverer" of natural selection, to see what socioeconomic growth had done to those trees: "We wound about among the hills and valleys, all perfectly dry," Wallace recalls in his autobiography, "till we reached a height of fifteen hundred feet, where many clumps of young redwoods were seen, and, stopping at one of these, Dr. Gibbons took me inside a circle of young trees . . . and showed me that they all grew on the outer edge of the huge charred trunk of an old tree that had been burnt down. This stump was thirty-four feet in diameter, or quite as large as the very largest of the more celebrated Big Trees, the *Sequoia gigantea*." (About the "Big Trees," Wallace wrote: "Of all the wonders I saw in America, nothing impressed me so much.")

In contrast to his wide explorations in the Sierra and Cascades, Muir more or less shunned the "redwood empire." His 1894 classic, *The Mountains of California*, devotes fourteen pages to the giant sequoia and two paragraphs to the coast redwood. (A map in the first edition doesn't even show mountains in northwestern California.) His journal account of a brief U.S. Forestry Commission inspection tour in 1896 bristles with suppressed anger: "Arrived Crescent City. Examined the mill and went out on a logging train a few miles and saw the work of ruin going on." And from another journal entry: "Any fool can destroy trees. . . . Nor can planting avail much toward restoring our grand aboriginal forests. It took more than three thousand years to make some of the oldest of the Sequoias. . . . Through all the eventful centuries since Christ's time, and long before that, God has cared for these trees, saved them from drought, disease, avalanches, and a thousand storms; but he cannot save them from sawmills and fools; this is left to the American people."

Muir's critique of progress was eccentric among Victorian-era naturalists, however. When he guided Asa Gray and another

Darwin associate, the English botanist Joseph Hooker, on treks to the mountains, the professionals sat silent by the campfire while the wild-eyed amateur extolled the forest's ageless glories and damned its destroyers. When asked why they seemed unimpressed, they said they liked to tease him. His attitude was extreme even among Victorian pantheists. Walt Whitman, who never saw a redwood forest, expressed a more typical fatalistic faith in progress in his "Song of the Redwood-Tree," a one-hundred-plus-line poem that is less about the tree than the socio-spiritual prospects of logging it:

> *A California Song! . . .*
> *Voice of a mighty dying tree in the Redwood forest dense. . . .*
>
> *My time has ended, my term has come. . . .*
>
> *At last the New arriving, assuming, taking possession. . . .*
> *Clearing the ground for broad humanity, the true America,*
> *heir of a*
> *past so grand*
>
> *To build a grander future.*

MEMORIAL GROVES

As it happened, the impetus to preserve at least some coast redwood time in public ownership arose more from Asa Gray's optimism than from Muir's cautionary pessimism. Despite sporadic logging, much of the Sierra's giant sequoia forest remained semi-protected in the public domain when Muir was active. Most of the coast's redwoods were passing into timber company hands, calling for a more pragmatic protection strategy than inclusion in big public-domain parks like Yosemite. Having grown up in a climate of vigorous if shortsighted progressivism, the naturalist generation that followed Gray and Muir proved ready for, if not altogether equal to, that challenge.

Of these, Henry Fairfield Osborn, a young ally of E. D. Cope in his bone wars with O. C. Marsh, was originally the most influential. Heir to a mercantile fortune, Osborn raised the "bone baron" category to that of "bone king" in a career that led from a Princeton professorship to presidency of the American Museum of Natural History. He also raised "progressivism" to "science" of a sort with an evolutionary sub-theory, "orthogenesis," that supplemented Darwin's natural selection with the notion that organisms have inherent tendencies to evolve in certain ways: to get bigger, for example, with the corollary that some might die out because they got too big and specialized to compete with newer, "fitter" species. Small, progressive mammals and oaks might have driven big, primitive dinosaurs and redwoods to extinction or relict status.

Osborn was not mainly a researcher, however. His chief talent was for using his museum to promote a kind of orthogenetic progress in civilization. This included now-discarded eugenics ideas but also more fruitful ones about how various kinds of public time claims might enhance quality of life. Osborn wanted to bring evolution's grandeur into the everyday world, and since redwoods are among its grandest manifestations, he early on devoted a "great hall" to them, popularizing Muir's exaltation of redwood venerability. The trunk section that intrigued me as a child may have been on a 1950s school field trip to his museum.

But displaying dead redwoods wasn't enough when living ones faced an industrial holocaust. Osborn got into national park issues when Muir was trying to stop San Francisco politicians from damming Yosemite's Hetch Hetchy Valley for a city reservoir, and Osborn was one of the few establishment bigwigs to support the beleaguered conservationist, who perhaps encouraged his own interest in redwoods. When Congress established the National Park Service in 1916, Osborn led two fellow progressives—Madison Grant and John C. Merriam—on an automotive odyssey into a redwood empire still so primitive that bad roads defeated their attempt to get from Eureka to Crescent City. The roads were good enough, however, that timber companies were cutting redwoods in

Humboldt County's remote Eel River canyons. To Madison Grant, president of the New York Zoological Society, the *un*progressiveness of this was self-evident:

> It is scarcely necessary to dwell on the crime involved in the destruction of the oldest and tallest trees on earth. . . . After the fall of the Roman Empire the priceless works of classic art were "needed" for lime, and statues. . . . were slacked down for this purpose, but the men who did it are today rightly dubbed "vandals and barbarians." What then will the next generation call us if we continue to destroy these priceless trees because lumber is "needed" for grape stakes and railroad ties?

The three wrote to Sacramento urging the creation of a park, but the government was unwilling to buy back swaths of what it had recently dropped from the public domain. So they joined with other progressives to start Save the Redwoods League, which took the more direct approach of acquiring parkland through donations. And they sold the idea as ownership of time more than space. Although Grant, a wilderness enthusiast, urged preserving the smaller conifer-hardwood forest of ridges along with big bottomland redwoods, the progressive priority was for saving as many grand old trees as possible. A popular way of doing so proved to be dedicating groves as "living monuments" to donors, which made time ownership not only a public benefaction but a private one that offered a kind of arboreal immortality. The resultant state parks largely protected roadside corridors, which was acceptable to local economies because it encouraged tourism and allowed logging outside the corridors.

The parks' success also arose from inexpensive brochures issued by the League. The most effective one consisted of John C. Merriam's "A Living Link in History" essay, which stayed in print for over five decades. As with Osborn, a sense of duty had impelled Merriam to move away from field and lab paleontology to a more public role, and in 1920 he left U.C. Berkeley to become president of the Carnegie Foundation in Washington, D.C. One possible reason for the brochure's lasting popularity was that "A Living Link" combined an administrator's progressive mystique with a naturalist's perception of the redwoods' beauty and age.

Frequent returns to the West kept Merriam involved with the League and led to his writing the essay. Standing among "living relics of distant ages" during one forest visit, he perceived not only the "clear story of a moving past" but "the future rising from it through the miracle of never-failing light." He went on to describe a private fossil exhibit, "The Petrified Forest," near Calistoga, where the trunks of huge trees "differing little" from living redwoods littered the ground. One display particularly impressed him: a tunnel into an "eight-foot-diameter log" buried under ashes and mud from a volcanic eruption three million years ago. Since that time, he wrote, "the flow of streams has been for ages carving the face of this land to its present form. Through all the time this shaping of the landscape was under way the prostrate 'Monarch' lay in quiet. . . . Only now and then there came a trembling of rocks around it. . . . And then the world of light returned, streams and wind flowed over it, living forests gathered round it, birds and beasts climbed again along its frame, and finally man came to see it, both as it is and as it was."

"A Living Link" contains a basic progressive idea: that time comes into full existence when the human mind perceives it. But this raises a problem in relation to evolutionary thinking. Such progressivism arose, at least implicitly, from the tradition that a "designing intelligence" created the conscious mind uniquely in humans—a tradition historically tied to millennial religious expectations that mind will transcend woody, bony natural or "fallen" time when it reunites with its celestial origins. (The innate progress of Osborn's orthogenesis theory was a pseudoscientific variant of this idea.) Yet Darwinism implies that mind originated in animals' nervous systems, not in unique divine creation, and evolutionary biology has yet to make much progress in understanding the relationship between nervous systems and mindful consciousness. Bears have complex nervous systems: does that make them conscious? Viewed in this light, Muir's timeless Sierra bears might be wishful thinking; bears may be more conscious of time than we know. "Advanced" as human consciousness may be, it doesn't allow us to experience bears' sense perceptions, much less their consciousness. And although mind may illuminate time, ancient plant fossils like those of redwoods show that it "marches on" whether perceived or not.

Merriam reveals uneasiness about evolution's implications for progressive ideas in another essay, "Are the Days of Creation Ended?" He writes: "We should have no sympathy with the suggestion that civilization is a disease which halts evolution and leads us to destruction. It is the natural development of human life, following the discovery and organization of knowledge. . . . There is nothing contributing to the support of our lives in a spiritual sense that seems so clearly indispensable as that which makes us look forward to continuing growth and improvement." Yet as "discovery and organization of knowledge" accelerate, along with "continuing growth and improvement," even until they begin to seem out of control, the idea of "natural development" gets more complicated.

SHIFTING CHRONOLOGIES

Pursuant to such uncertainties, evolutionist progressivism had been unraveling for a decade when Merriam wrote "A Living Link." One of its tenets had been Lord Kelvin's 1866 estimate, based on the rate of cooling from an original molten state, that the earth is around 100 million years old. This assessment virtually mandated rapid progress for life, with the entire age of mammals squeezed into the last 2 million years. But in 1903, another physicist, Lord Rayleigh, showed that radioactivity in the earth's core counteracts Kelvin's cooling effect, and by the 1920s geologists had developed dating techniques showing that multicellular organisms have existed for at least 500 million years.

The new time scale suggested that redwoods have existed in something like their present form not just for the impressive 10 million years of Kelvin's scheme but for a staggering 130 million years. The innate progress of Osborn's orthogenesis sank without a ripple in this new temporal ocean, while Darwin's gradual process of natural selection, which Kelvin's scheme had obscured, returned to the theoretical surface. Mammals and oaks might have predominated over dinosaurs and redwoods not because they were more "advanced" but because they were luckier—more fortuitously adapted to climatic or geological changes. Likewise, dinosaurs and redwoods might have predominated for millions of years before mammals and oaks because of similar fortuitous adaptations.

Surprising new evidence of fortuitous adaptions in redwoods emerged a decade after Merriam's "Living Link" brochure came out. It turned out that the sequoias that "flourished throughout the polar regions" during the Cretaceous and Tertiary periods weren't as similar to living ones as Asa Gray had thought. In 1941, Japanese botanists determined from Asian Cretaceous fossils that a redwood genus once thought to be *Sequoia* was quite different, with sprays of deciduous needles more like those of the related bald cypress than the redwood. They named it *Metasequoia*, often called the "dawn redwood." In 1946, Chinese botanists found a living *Metasequoia* at a temple in the central province of Szechuan. Two years later, Ralph W. Chaney, who had succeeded Merriam as Berkeley's professor of paleontology, went to Szechuan, traveling inland from the Yangtze River for three days on footpaths, and saw the "enormous" temple tree, along with other *Metasequoia* specimens. Farming had obliterated the native forest locally, so he walked south into the hills for another 115 miles and finally found the trees growing in ravines: "It was these trees which I had crossed the Pacific and much of China to see, so that I might reconstruct and visualize the forests of ages past," Chaney exulted. "And I was not disappointed. Growing beside the dawn redwoods in the village of Shiu-hsa-pa, at an altitude of about 4,000 feet, were birches, chestnuts, sweet gums, beeches, oaks, and at least one large katsura [a solely Asian hardwood]. The Arcto-Tertiary Flora was growing there before me, with essentially the same membership as the group which had its origin to the north millions of years before, and which migrated southward down both sides of the Pacific."

Finding *Metasequoia* in a deciduous forest unlike the largely evergreen ones inhabited by *Sequoia* and *Sequoiaden-*

dron, Chaney surmised that it had adapted along with its angiosperm associates to a dinosaur-age Arctic that, despite having a warmer climate than today's, also must have undergone months of total darkness in winter. When he later examined the Arctic fossils that Gray had attributed to *Sequoia*, he found that almost all were *Metasequoia*. So the newly discovered genus was less a product of evolutionary progress than a relic of a "lost world" that the cooling, drying global climate had almost obliterated. From this unprogressive viewpoint, the same was true of *Metasequoia*'s living relatives, *Sequoia* and *Sequoiadendron*, whose ancestors grew with it in places like Yellowstone, where conditions were less extreme than in the Arctic. They too were much-reduced survivors on an earth that, with the recent spread of the sparser, lower-growing flora of grasslands, deserts, and tundra, seems much more a product of random chance than of upward advancement.

GROWTH AND STABILITY

The twentieth century's world wars and other disasters projected the newly chancy version of evolutionary time onto historic time. Post–World War II conservationists like David Brower still believed in civilized progress, but they associated it less with socioeconomic growth and more with new biological concepts like ecological stability and species diversity. This coincided with growing public anxiety as pollution, resource depletion, and other impacts of growth intensified, leading to the environmentalist view that the public should own and protect significant continuums of natural ecosystems and species—big swaths of evolutionary time as well as space—to maintain a healthy biosphere.

Growth was impacting old-growth redwoods catastrophically. After the timber industry logged the watersheds above the redwood state parks, disastrous floods erupted in the 1950s, undermining and sweeping away hundreds of expensively preserved monuments to progress. Schizoid between growth and stability, 1960s society went into dual overdrive as industrialists raced to cut as much original coast redwood forest as possible while environmentalists raced to save as much as possible.

"Tall and straight the last redwoods stand, while we debate their fate," writes François Leydet, author of *The Last Redwoods*, a 1963 exemplar of the influential "exhibit format" books that the Sierra Club published under Brower's leadership. "It is somehow preposterous that we of this generation—we of this decade even—should have the power to reprieve or condemn a race that nature has preserved over one hundred million years. There is something frighteningly presumptuous about a man, his life span limited to a few decades, who strides up to a redwood that has seen a thousand summers and might see as many more, and in an hour's hacking and sawing brings the giant down."

The race centered on the Redwood Creek gorge, a 240,000-acre watershed between Eureka and Crescent City originally so remote that Madison Grant proposed it as a national park in 1920. Even though Grant's proposal failed, logging didn't get well under way there until the 1950s, but by then technology was so efficient that the whole watershed could have become a clear-cut moonscape in a few years. Environmentalists were able to rush a Redwood Creek Unit of a new Redwood National Park through Congress in 1968, but it protected only 20,000 acres of the watershed's original forest. Industry logged the rest, and post-logging floods smothered the creek in gravel and silt, decimating the once outstanding salmonid spawning populations.

Although the Mill Creek Unit of the new multiunit national park also saved much old growth around Crescent City, it was not as integral as that on Redwood Creek. There went the dream that at least one unlogged watershed of *Sequoia*'s original range might remain completely in redwood time as a monument to evolutionary stability. And it remains hard to get more protection for the remaining coast redwood ancient forests. When pro-environment president Bill Clinton left office in 2000, his legacy included a new national monument for the Sierra's sequoias, but not for the coast's. President Barack Obama did proclaim a roughly 5,800-acre Santa Cruz Redwoods National Monument on the central coast in 2017, but only part of that is redwood old growth, and incorporating it into the national park system will take a while.

Ideally, coast redwood protection might take an example from the giant sequoia protection that Muir and his successors carried out. They did it by protecting not just the sequoia groves themselves but the transects of ancient conifer forest, from the Sierra foothills to the Nevada and Mojave deserts, contained in Yosemite, Sequoia, and Kings Canyon national parks. Admittedly, transects of coastal conifer forest would be much harder to protect today, but possibilities exist at the south and north extents of coast redwoods' range. At Big Sur, the big trees on the coast could connect with the smaller redwoods that extend up the canyons to the Ventana Wilderness's unique montane forest of Santa Lucia fir and ponderosa. At Crescent City, the supremely diverse redwood forest of the Mill Creek and Jedidiah Smith units could connect with the Siskiyou Wilderness's unique montane forest of Brewer's spruce, Port Orford cedar, Alaska yellow cedar, and many other species. The Forest Service has logged and roaded the Douglas fir and hardwood forest of the steep slopes between them, but the slopes are so steep that the roads keep falling down. Perhaps, in some future political climate friendlier to ecology than today's, new "transectual" parks might be created in those places.

TIME WARPS

The old naturalists like Gray and Muir would have trouble fitting their largely continuous notions of time to today's existing coast redwood parks. If any one word could describe redwood time now, it would not be either "cyclic" or "progressive" but, perhaps, "broken." Gray and Muir envisioned the public contemplating a landscape accessible by foot or horse, but Osborn and Merriam unwittingly initiated some parks where ancient redwood groves stand within sight or sound of car traffic that gets thicker and faster every year, rendering the world's tallest trees less objects of reverence and awe than blurs out the windshield or shade for littered pit stops. Even in a large state park like Prairie Creek, where one can walk through old growth for hours, there is an awareness of fragmentation, an expectation that "the end is near."

Strange time warps occur in these surroundings. I once stopped along Highway 101 where it runs through the national park south of Crescent City to admire some lilies, and as I stepped from the car, a small animal ran underneath. I first thought it was a lizard, but it was a shrew, a rarer sight. It seemed lost, cowering under the muffler, and I felt the uneasy pity that arises when a wild animal wanders into the technological spotlight. But then it ran back into the forest and I decided that my pity was deluded. The shrew came from a continuum of redwood-forest small mammals that goes back to the Jurassic period, so it wasn't at all clear who had a more privileged place in "time's living currents," it or me.

Standing miles from a road on Redwood Creek, where a black bear can snooze for hours undisturbed in a sunny glade, I have felt that I was in unbroken redwood time. But something dispels the illusion: perhaps the lifelessness of the silt-smothered creek, or the sound of bulldozers from the slopes above, where the Park Service works to restore logged areas by removing old roads and culverts that keep eroding the slopes and sending more silt into the creek. In 1978, Congress enlarged the park by 48,000 acres to include some of the logged area, and it directed the Park Service to restore ecological damage, but that proved easier said than done. When restorers planted trees, new floods just washed them away. Eventually they discovered that the same heavy earthmover technology that carved out the logging roads and culverts was necessary to rebuild the slopes' contours so that winter rains would run off less destructively.

Restoration seems to me a bit like running a film of dynamiting backward, allowing the exploded objects to "reassemble." This can look magically comic on film, but forest restoration is much slower than logging, not at all magical, and there is nothing comic about it except the irony that it uses the same technology as logging. And some things can't be restored with bulldozers. The flood silt that smothers Redwood Creek will have to work its way down and out of the waterway's mouth through natural stream flow before significant salmon spawning can return, and it may take longer for native fish populations to recover from their present reduced numbers.

Trying to restore even a small piece of unbroken redwood time can seem quixotic in a society committed to growth. It can imply a kind of hubris, as when, in response to the narrator's warning that "you can't repeat the past," the tragic hero of F. Scott Fitzgerald's *The Great Gatsby* cries, "Why of course you can!" Yet if there is hubris in Jay Gatsby's cry, there may be more in the truism to which he responds. Narrator Nick Carraway's "you can't repeat the past" echoes Walt Whitman's fatalistic heralding of a "grander future" in "The Song of the Redwood-Tree." By supplanting the giants, Whitman implies, civilization inevitably will assume their majesty and venerability. History shows, however, that assumptions of "continuing growth and improvement" are problematic as civilizations rise and fall. California poet Robinson Jeffers, Whitman's pessimistic antithesis, likens socioeconomic growth to a "double axe" in his ten-line poem "Science." The metaphor seems apt in the case of redwood forest:

> *Man, introverted man . . .*
> *Now he's bred knives on nature turns them also inward:*
> *they*
> *Have thirsty points . . .*

CONSERVATION BIOLOGY

In reality, anyway, the giants are not supplanted. The coast redwood remains among the more resilient tree species, still occupying most of its pre-Columbian range as second or third growth. Logged giants re-sprout from root burls, continuing clonal lives that extend immeasurably into the past. Seed-grown trees mature quickly, soon producing vast numbers of seedlings that compete effectively with plant rivals. Mature trees have exceptionally long lives because they are exceptionally resistant to pests, disease, fire, and drought; presumably, the genus has had a long evolutionary life for similar reasons. Within its environmental limits—mild winters, high seasonal rainfall, adequate soil moisture—the coast redwood dominates forests wherein it occurs.

Biologically, the forest's "woody stasis" is an illusion of limited human perception. Science has found plenty of "natural development" in redwood time, particularly in the intricate microbial relationships that keep the forest alive and healthy. Hundreds of fungal and bacterial species living in the soil and on roots enable trees to absorb water and nutrients efficiently. Indeed, temperate old-growth conifer forests may have the most diverse soil ecosystems on earth. Some microbes live inside the trees, like the tiny fungus with the big name—*Pleuroplaconema*—that colonizes redwood needles and stems and evidently protects them from disease. Research has shown that redwoods colonized by the fungus are largely free of infections, while over 95 percent of uncolonized trees have some kind of infection. The fungus apparently produces toxins that repel insect pests and disease organisms by making the plant tissues unpalatable or poisonous. Botanists speculate that the fungus originally was a redwood parasite, which then evolved a more "mutualistic" relationship with the trees. Such evolution proceeds continually throughout the forest, and we still know little about it.

The larger life of the forest is less uniquely diverse, but equally complex, from the marbled murrelets, condors, and eagles that nest in the treetops; to the tree voles and clouded salamanders that inhabit mini-forests of ferns, shrubs, and even young trees growing epiphytically on the giant trees' branches; to the spotted owls, Pacific fishers, Humboldt martens, and Humboldt's flying squirrels (recently deemed a new species) of the understories; to the Olympic and Pacific giant salamanders that live underground and breed in springs. Many of these species are too small, cryptic, or rare for everyday sighting, but even the forest's more conspicuous biodiversity goes far beyond the "woody stasis" of casual impressions. Redwoods, ferns, and mosses may seem monotonous, but many other plant species comprise the forest, and the flora gets increasingly diverse toward the North Coast heart of *Sequoia*'s range. Douglas firs grow nearly as tall as redwoods there, while Sitka spruce, western hemlock, grand fir, and western redcedar join the two giant conifer species to form an emergent canopy over trees like western yew, tanoak, golden chinquapin, coast live oak, madrone, bigleaf maple, red alder, and western ash. Equally diverse are shrubs like hazel, azalea, rhododendron, huckleberry, and salmonberry, and wildflowers and other herbaceous angiosperms.

The biodiversity is not only in the forest itself. Redwoods have been coevolving with fish for as long as with mammals, and the relationship probably has been particularly close with anadromous species like salmon. The quantity of nutrients that salmon bring into watersheds as they spawn and die may affect soil fertility and, perhaps, the size of stream-bottom trees.

Nobody knows just why redwoods get so tall, and there are many factors at work, but soil fertility must be one. In the 1870s, bone baron O. C. Marsh found a fossil species in the Bay Area now called the sabertoothed salmon, partly because it had long canine teeth (used in mating displays) like the also-extinct saber-toothed cat, and also because it was "prehistorically" large—twice the size of living king salmon. Redwoods grew in the Bay Area a few million years ago, when five-foot-long sabertoothed salmon spawned there. Given the historically supreme size of the Oakland Hills trees, those Miocene-epoch redwoods might have matched sabertoothed salmon in magnitude. No known living redwood attains a height of four hundred feet, much less five hundred, but are such heights impossible?

Restoration is as much about perpetuating the biodiversity

that 130 million years of evolution have imbued in the forest as it is protecting the big trees of preserves. While early scientists like Gray were mainly interested in describing the natural world, later ones like Chaney were increasingly concerned with perpetuating it, with the help of what has become known as "conservation biology." (On his return from China, Chaney worked to get dawn redwoods planted in arboretums and other venues worldwide, a measure that was already under way with the coast redwood and giant sequoia.) A basic tenet of conservation biology is that while pristine parks are vital, they aren't enough to perpetuate biodiversity if they are preserved in isolation while other lands are stripped of native flora and fauna. According to the well-documented "island effect," even the most pristine preserves will steadily lose species in isolation as disease, natural disaster, and other factors wipe out native populations that aren't replaced by immigration from surrounding lands. Conservationists increasingly try to link preserves with systems of less pristine but still natural land that allow biodiversity to keep flowing.

To give an example of restoration's problems and potentials, some of the devastated forest that Alfred Russell Wallace saw in 1886 has regrown in Redwood Regional Park, opened in 1939, which now covers 1,803 acres of the Oakland Hills. The park's forest is certainly not pristine, and many problems persist. The "clumps of young redwoods" that Wallace described were logged again after the 1906 earthquake, making the park's forest a third-growth one, and much biodiversity has been lost. (The overall flora is poorer than in old-growth forests.) Also, the land there hasn't been restored as in Redwood National Park; old skid roads used to drag out logs with ox teams are still discernible on the slopes of Redwood Regional. Further, aquatic life in the park's own Redwood Creek is threatened, including a native trout population. And the East Bay's redwood stands aren't adjacent to other redwood forests, a circumstance that falls short of the conservation biology goal of connecting habitats in "biodiversity corridors" that will allow species to flow back and forth.

The East Bay redwoods apparently were already isolated from other stands when Europeans arrived, however, and adjacent conservation areas do connect them with other natural habitats such as oak woodland and chaparral. Even somewhat isolated natural areas can provide habitat for airborne migratory species like insects and birds, and they can protect a lot of residual biodiversity. I've found John Muir's favorite wildflower species, the reclusive calypso orchid, in the Oakland park. And the recovering forest still manifests some of the grandeur and venerability Merriam evokes in "A Living Link"—the hypnotic interplays of light and shade, the sense of eddying time. Many of today's trees are stump-sprouts and thus genetic clones of the ancient trees. As long as the park is protected adequately, the Oakland forest will become more biodiverse as the trees grow and harbor more life.

DISTANT EPOCHS

Despite hopeful measures, over 95 percent of coast redwood old growth is gone, and much land that once supported redwood forest doesn't anymore, as in the Oakland Hills. So what of Walt Whitman's "grander future"? The freeways, monster homes, and mini-malls that now surround Redwood Regional Park might have pleased him, but they don't seem all that grand from his progressive viewpoint. The ingrained rural poverty that Ralph W. Chaney encountered while searching for near-extinct *Metasequoia* among the "broad humanity" of war-torn 1940s China certainly would not have pleased the expansive poet, and in 1967 Chaney voiced what might be a saner forecast of "redwood futures": "We are fortunate to be living on earth before many of the genera of the Arcto-Tertiary Geoflora have disappeared, while even those on the verge of extinction can be seen and studied. And when they are gone in some distant epoch of earth history, it will be a rewarding experience for earth scientists and botanists of tomorrow to discover, and to view with understanding eyes, the trees that have come to fill vacant niches in the geoflora of the future."

Admittedly, those geologists and botanists of "some distant epoch" seem tenuous. How distant? Enough for new redwood species to evolve? It's hard to imagine people who won't observe the speed limit waiting for that. The busy freeway just west of Redwood Regional Park, Highway 13, overlies the massive Hayward Fault, threatening an explosive short-term future for Bay Area humans, and it is just one of many threats to "civilized time." Also, Chaney made his forecast before climate change became an issue; who knows what will happen as mass consumption of fossil fuels raises the planet's temperature? A probable warming, drying climate does not bode well for America's two sequoia species. Ideal conditions for them, both in the Sierra and on the coast, will shift upward and northward, and it is not clear whether species that live for such long time spans will be able to adapt during the next few centuries. The future could be grim for the peripheral, Ent-like redwoods I found in the Ventana Wilderness, which may have needed many centuries to grow to their relatively small size in their marginal surroundings.

Yet civilization can't keep growing and emitting greenhouse gases forever on a finite planet. Scientific studies like the Club of Rome's computer-generated 1975 report *The Limits to Growth* predict global socioeconomic collapse from pollution and resource depletion within the end of this century. Even several more centuries of continued economic growth might not make that much difference to tree species that measure their individual life spans in millennia. Mathematical probability theory says that what has lasted longest is likely to last longest. Maybe, if the climate keeps warming, ice caps melt, and oceans rise to flood continents, what Gray and Chaney called the Arcto-Tertiary Geoflora will stop disappearing and reoccupy its former range from Greenland and Siberia to Europe and Yellowstone. Maybe Charles Lyell will prove right after all, and some re-evolved pterodactyl-like creature will "flit again through the umbrageous groves" of redwood descendants. Some ecologically inclined future civilization might set genetically cloned brontosaurs to browsing redwoods in Jurassic Parks. As dimensions go, time is starting to look friendlier than space. Given known science's paradigm of a hostile solar system and unimaginably vast universe, we may not be able to travel far in space, but we might be able to "travel" far in time if our descendants can survive that long.

But redwood time is not all so distant and speculative. I perhaps exaggerated when I described sleeping with the Ventana Wilderness redwoods as a unique plunge into that state of being. In fact, I sleep with coast redwoods every night; they grow all over my Berkeley neighborhood, along with some giant sequoias and dawn redwoods. This was not *Sequoia* forest originally—the trees must have grown from nursery seedlings since the area suburbanized in the early 1900s—yet some coast redwoods here are bigger than the genetically ancient stump-sprout clones in Redwood Regional Park. A massive one towers above the next house over, scattering twigs and cones on my roof, sometimes blocking the gutters. Young redwoods grow fast.

DAVID RAINS WALLACE *has published over twenty books about natural history and conservation, including* The Klamath Knot, *a study of northwestern California ecology and evolution, which won the John Burroughs Medal for Nature Writing in 1984.*

RELATED TITLES

The Forests of California, by Obi Kaufmann

From the author of *The California Field Atlas* (#1 San Francisco Chronicle Best Seller) comes a major work that not only guides readers through the Golden State's forested lands but also presents a profoundly original vision of nature in the twenty-first century. *The Forests of California* features an abundance of Obi Kaufmann's signature watercolor maps and trail paintings, weaving them into an expansive and accessible exploration of the biodiversity that defines California in the global imagination. ISBN: 978-1-59714-479-7

King Sequoia: The Tree That Inspired a Nation, Created Our National Park System, and Changed the Way We Think about Nature, by William C. Tweed

Former park ranger William C. Tweed takes readers on a tour of the Big Trees and reveals how one tree species has transformed Americans' connection to the natural world. When sequoias, which seemed to embody California's superlative appeal, were threatened by logging interests, the feelings of horror that this desecration evoked in people catalyzed protection efforts that directly inspired the Park Idea. Then as science evolved to consider landscapes more holistically, sequoias were once again at the heart of an attitudinal shift. ISBN: 978-1-59714-351-6

The Last Stand: The War Between Wall Street and Main Street over California's Ancient Redwoods, by David Harris

This "gripping and informative" (*Publishers Weekly*) account of financier Charles Hurwitz's takeover of the Pacific Lumber Company in remote Northern California is as much a story about the struggle for the soul of capitalism as it is about the fight to save the ancient redwoods on the company's lands. For generations the family-owned company operated under the principle of long-term sustainability over short-term profits. With a journalist's astute eye for detail and an activist's moral outrage, David Harris chronicles the drastic changes that came as a result of a buyout by a Texas-based conglomerate, whose greed-fueled destruction of the redwoods ultimately doomed the enterprise. ISBN: 978-1-59714-441-4

Trees in Paradise: The Botanical Conquest of California, by Jared Farmer

At the intersection of plants and politics, *Trees in Paradise* is an examination of ecological mythmaking and conquest. The first Americans in California remade the landscape according to their own aesthetic values and economic interests. In Southern California, entrepreneurs amassed fortunes from vast citrus groves; in the Bay Area, gum trees planted to beautify neighborhoods fed wildfires; and across the state, the palm came to stand for the ease and luxury of the rapidly expanding suburbs. Meanwhile, thousands of native redwoods and sequoias were logged to satisfy the insatiable urbanizing impulse. This natural and unnatural history unravels the network of forces that shape our most fundamental sense of place. ISBN: 978-1-59714-392-9